PROJECT KEEPSAKE

PROJECT KEEPSAKE

An Anthology

Amber Lanier Nagle
and Friends

INTEGRATED MEDIA
NEW YORK

All rights reserved, including without limitation the right to reproduce this book or any portion thereof in any form or by any means, whether electronic or mechanical, now known or hereinafter invented, without the express written permission of the publisher.

Copyright © 2014 by Amber Lanier Nagle

ISBN: 978-1-5040-7943-3

This edition published in 2023 by Open Road Integrated Media, Inc.
180 Maiden Lane
New York, NY 10038
www.openroadmedia.com

CONTENTS

INTRODUCTION	xi
HERMAN'S BROWN BUCKEYES by Amber Lanier Nagle	1
UNCLE JAMES' POCKET KNIFE by Renea Winchester	6
MY BELOVED MIXING BOWL: "BIG GREEN" by Marcia M. Swearingen	10
BIRDIE B.'S SILVER SCISSORS by Sharon Huey	14
MY FATHER'S FOUNTAIN PEN by Estelle Rodis-Brown	20
THE PREGNANCY SHIRT by Coleen Brooks	26
THE EASTMAN CHEMICAL TANK CAR by Paul Garrison	31
THE CUSTARD SPOON by Jean Lowrey	41

CONTENTS

HARRY AFT'S SIGNET RING by David Aft	45
THE BRICK by Wayne Minshew	49
A TALE OF TWO CLOCKS by Martha Ford Fry	52
GRANDMA LISSIE'S DEVIL'S EAR by Sherry Poff	59
THE BOOK by Dorothy McCrory	64
BLUE PLATE SPECIAL by Jane Starner	67
CARNIVAL GLASS by Nancy Ratcliffe	71
THE PICTURE HAT by Janie Dempsey Watts	76
JONATHAN'S BIBLE AND MARGARET'S WAX VINE by Jim Gilreath	80
UNDEFEATED: THE CAST by Peggy Gilbert	86
NANNY'S MAGIC PAN by Mitzi Boyd	91
LUCKY LOTTERY NUMBERS by Audrey Lanier Andersen	95
THE BEANIE BABIES by Rachel Brown	102
GRANDPA'S POCKET WATCH by Dick Aft	105
GRANDMA AND GRANDPA: CUSTODY OF THE FIGURINES by Phyllis Qualls Freeman	109

CONTENTS

DOWNED BIRD by Joanne Crockett Lewis	113
MY GRANDMA'S UGLY QUILTS by Barbara Tucker	116
MY MOTHER'S GUITAR by Bob Wright	120
A STASH OF SHINY SILVER DOLLARS by Dana Cooley-Keith	124
PINK ANGEL by Lois Baldwin Good	127
THE PIE PLATE by Karen H. Phillips	132
THE MUSIC BOX by Mariah Fulton	136
THE QUILL by Chris Foster	140
THE OLD SINGER SEWING MACHINE by Amber Lanier Nagle	150
MY GRANDMOTHER'S PILL BOX HAT by Pauline Melton	156
MAMA'S GOLD BANGLE BRACELET by Priscilla N. Shartle	160
COUSIN GERALDINE'S WATCH by Judy Peterson	165
TOM SENIOR'S WALLET AND CELL PHONE by Tom Durkan	170
AUNT DORIS' RED CROSS PIN by Mary Lu Aft	174

CONTENTS

A BLESSING AROUND MY FINGER by Cynthia Wilson	178
DAD'S DRESSER by Julie Moss	182
GRANNY ROSIE'S ORGAN AND MILKING STOOL by Jesse Vaughn	187
PIECES OF ESNOMS-AU-VAL by Francine Fuqua	193
MY TIN SEWING KIT by Victoria R. Choate	201
GRANDMA'S BANDS OF GOLD by Christine Alexander Jennison	205
THE FARM TABLE by Marvin Lewis	210
THE OLD CRANK TELEPHONE by Phyllis Qualls Freeman	213
MATTIE BELL'S BIBLE by Missionary Janie Aker	217
MEMENTOS OF A FREEMASON by Ken Berry	221
THE OLD IRON BED by Martha Buttrum	232
CIRCUS TEDDY BEAR by Elizabeth Swafford	235
THE RUBBER STAMP by Tim Egenes	242
THE BLUE DIARY by Shannon Lucadano	245
JEMARIS' PURPLE CUP by Carmen Slaughter	248

CONTENTS

THE LINDE STAR NECKLACE by Thelma J. Benner	252
CASTANETS by Debbie Dickson	256
WRITING ABOUT KEEPSAKES	261
WITH SINCERE GRATITUDE	275
ABOUT THE EDITOR	277

INTRODUCTION

A few years ago, I watched a prime time television special featuring the president and first lady touring a reporter around the White House. They paused in each room and pointed to a vase, a piece of furniture, a painting, or a sculpture and relayed the history of each object to viewers—where the item came from, what year it was added to the White House collection, and its significance.

I had never been particularly interested in the house at 1600 Pennsylvania Avenue, its furnishings, grandeur, or history, yet that night, the story behind each piece drew me in and held me captive.

The following day, I surveyed my own home, room by room. I started in the dining room where a small plank of wood hung on the wall—a crude image of the Virgin Mary cradling Jesus in her arms painted on its surface in muted maroons, burgundies, and golds. My husband and I purchased the piece from a street vendor in Athens, Greece just a few years before. It reminded us of the colorful frescos we had seen painted on walls and ceilings of various churches and religious landmarks throughout the city, and so we bought it as a souvenir—to help us remember the fun we shared as we explored ancient Greek ruins on our first trip abroad.

INTRODUCTION

In the center of our dining room, we had positioned a beefy oak pedestal table under a crystal chandelier. Again, memories flooded my mind. We bought the table from an antique dealer in Byron, Georgia. My in-laws were with us that day, and even though it was scratched and blemished, we fell in love with the craftsman style table. We haggled a little with the dealer and eventually bought the piece at what we considered a steal. Together, the four of us witnessed the table's grand entrance into our first home—such a happy memory.

I walked into our kitchen and noticed a set of four handmade ceramic canisters my mother had made and given us as a wedding gift. In my mind's eye, I saw Mom hunched over the raw pieces as she sanded, painted and glazed each canister and lid. She carved her name and the date on the bottom of each piece so we would always remember she had made them for us, but how could we ever forget? And how could I ever forget the moments Mom and I shared working on ceramics together at the kitchen table as I grew up?

Walking into the guest bedroom, I was greeted by a wooden dresser and chest of drawers. The furniture had belonged to my great-grandparents. In the seventies, someone had painted the pieces an ugly avocado green. I hated the color, but I felt a strong attachment to the heirlooms and vowed to refinish them and restore them to their original glory. I loved the idea of touching and using items my great-grandparents had touched and used.

Ten minutes into my journey, I realized that our house—like the White House—brimmed with keepsakes and mementoes. Every piece induced a memory of a person, a place, or a special moment. My husband and I were, and still are, caretakers of these items and others—we are devout memory keepers. And each time we move, we carefully pack our keepsakes, haul

INTRODUCTION

them across Georgia, and place them in prominent spots in our new home.

Each day, these items sing memories to me. The crocheted afghan in my upstairs closet sings about my maternal grandmother's wrinkled hands weaving it into existence. A pinkish, purplish vase hanging in my office hums about how much my in-laws enjoyed shopping at estate sales in areas of Chattanooga known for their old money. An old tin, wind-up toy sings a song of a German Shepherd it once terrorized as it rolled around in a circle beneath the dog's paws. A large, oak rocker sings a song of my father's mother rocking while reading letters she received from a lonely hearts club.

In today's world, our homes are museums of our lives, and we are but curators presiding over dozens of objects that meet the definition of keepsake, memento, heirloom, or souvenir. Whether we display our items in curio cabinets or tuck them away in shoeboxes underneath our beds, the appeal is not in their physical being, but in the stories and memories they represent to each of us.

"Why do you keep this?" I ask when I visit friends' homes.

And then I listen as the stories and memories pour out. Each keepsake—each story—is unique, yet each reveals a commonality that resonates with all of us and celebrates the shared experience of humanity.

My revelation is simple: everyone has a keepsake, and every keepsake has a story to tell. And so I launched *Project Keepsake*—my quest to collect and publish the stories behind people's cherished keepsakes.

At one point, I considered writing a collection of stories about my own keepsakes and treasures or composing other peoples' stories myself, but I feared my renditions would lack authenticity and fail to capture the depth and unique perspective of

INTRODUCTION

each item. The keepers' own words convey the feelings and emotions much better than my interpretations could. So, I encouraged others to explore the deep-rooted connections they have to their own keepsakes and mementos and write about them. For those who were hesitant to write their own, I offered to help them, but only after they drafted their story themselves.

Most mornings, I wake to find messages or even better, draft stories, in my inbox. For me, reading the stories is like unwrapping a very personal gift. Through their stories, the contributors allow me to peek into their hearts and souls, and sometimes, like a reflection in a mirror, I see myself.

As of today, the collection includes over fifty-five complete stories told in first-person by people with very different backgrounds and writing styles, and several other contributors are in the process of writing and editing their stories. Each story is uplifting. Each is transcendent. Each is beautiful. Each is sacred.

I am proud that *Project Keepsake* provides an outlet to celebrate these very special stories and memories and the very human journeys that connect us all.

While I have learned many things from *Project Keepsake*, one lesson that presents itself over and over again is that all of us keep and hold onto objects that link us to the memories we care most about. We keep things so that we will remember, but somewhere along the way, these keepsakes take on a life of their own and define where we came from, what matters to us, and perhaps most of all, who we are.

—*Amber Lanier Nagle,*
October 2012

HERMAN'S BROWN BUCKEYES

AMBER LANIER NAGLE

I sat curled-up in a ball on the sofa watching television when Daddy strolled in and collapsed into the black vinyl cushions of his favorite recliner. He exhaled heavily with a breathy "Whooey," at the end and set a glass of bourbon and Coke on a nearby coaster.

His manly aroma floated across the room, and I breathed it in—a mixture of deer blood, alcohol, sweat, and cigarette smoke—an earthy smell that, to this day, reminds me of Daddy. He had spent the majority of the weekend with his buddies at K&G Hunting Club just outside of Lizella, Georgia doing whatever he and the other men did out there.

"What does he do at the hunting club?" I often asked my mother.

"Oh, I don't know," Mom said. "Walk around, look for deer tracks, build deer hunting stands, pull trucks out of the mud, drink too much and gamble next to the campfire with the other men. Your father finds refuge in being outdoors."

My dad, Herman Franklin Lanier, worked two jobs to support our family of five. He supervised an air freight terminal at a local Air Force base and installed trailer hitches on vehicles at a business in Macon that he owned with my Uncle Edwin. But many weekends—especially when there was a hint of fall in the air—Daddy retreated to the woods to recharge his batteries.

I looked over at him that day. He wore a dirty camouflage shirt, a cap, tattered jeans, and an old pair of black sneakers with clots of dried mud hanging on the soles. Mom would be upset when the dirt fell onto her clean linoleum floor later that evening. He kneaded his neck for a few strokes and let out a heavy sigh before emptying the weekend's souvenirs from his pockets—a few loose coins, a broken piece of chalky peppermint, a pocketknife, the tip of an arrowhead, and two buckeyes.

He tossed a buckeye over to me, and I caught it in my right hand. He grinned and said, "Keep it. It'll bring you good luck."

Daddy was not a superstitious man, but during the years of my childhood, he handed me dozens of buckeyes he had retrieved from the forest's floor, always followed by the promise of good fortune. I hoarded the shiny, brown nuggets for years keeping them in a jewelry box protected by a tiny, twirling ballerina, and I had a pretty lucky childhood, so I had no reason to doubt the mysterious power of buckeyes. I was a true-blue buckeye believer.

As a young adult, I stashed them everywhere—in the side panels of my pocketbooks, in the belly drawer of my desk, in the glove compartment of my car, and in the pockets of my coats and jackets. After a while, the buckeyes reminded me less and less of luck and fortune, and more and more of my father and his lifelong love of all things outdoors—hunting, fishing, sitting by a glowing campfire, and roaming the backwoods of Georgia on foot.

As I grew older, I grew away from my childhood passions and possessions, and like most people do, I grew away from my parents a bit, too. I eventually packed the dolls and toys that populated my childhood away neatly in boxes, and I stopped collecting buckeyes. They just weren't a priority any more.

Then in August of 1992, Daddy died. He was here one day, and the next day, he was simply *gone*. Mom, my siblings and I gathered to mourn and plan his funeral and burial, all the while wondering and guessing what he would have wanted.

Mom finally decided to bury Daddy in a pair of denim jeans and a flannel shirt. "That's what he was most comfortable wearing," she said, and Andy, Audrey, and I agreed.

The four of us drove to the funeral home that evening to view Daddy's body privately. I've never felt as broken as when I saw my father's lifeless body lying in that casket. I was terrified that I would eventually forget what he looked like, so I scrutinized every detail of his face—every wrinkle and every scar—and burned his image to my memory. His graying hair was missing on top of his head, and his nose was large and bony—a replica of my own nose, but with a web of broken blood vessels that come with age.

The flannel shirt we had selected for him had a pocket on the left-hand side. "Herman always had to have a pocket on his shirts," Mom remarked that night, standing at his side. "He had to have a place to put those damned cigarettes."

But there were no cigarettes that night. The pocket was oddly empty, and that's when I had the idea: to honor my father, I would place a buckeye in his shirt pocket.

At home that night, I searched high and low for a nice, round buckeye to tuck in Daddy's pocket prior to the funeral. I fumbled through the contents of the junk drawer in our kitchen—no buckeye. I fell on the floor of my closet and opened a dusty shoebox of miscellaneous trinkets—still, no buckeye. Coat pockets—empty. Car console—nothing.

I called my mother and relayed my dilemma to her. She comforted me and told me not to worry about it, but my heart collapsed. In a lifetime of being surrounded by Daddy's buckeyes, how could I not find even *one* in the hiding places of my life? I felt ashamed—as if I had failed him in some way.

The following day, friends and family members congregated at the funeral home to pay their final respects. The experience was surreal. Daddy's open casket rested at the front of the room illuminated by a dozen tiny spotlights and surrounded by elaborate flower arrangements and potted peace lilies. People mingled as if it were a cocktail party occasionally working their way over to my father's figure. It was as if Daddy were sleeping in the middle of a social gathering.

Mom's best friend, Nita, approached me with a consoling smile, then hugged me tightly. She took my hand and dropped something into it. One of the smooth, mahogany nuggets so familiar to me—so dear to my heart—rested on the flat surface of my palm. I stared at the beautiful, unblemished buckeye as if it was a chunk of gold then glanced up at her face.

"Your mama told me that you were looking for one of these," Nita said. "My daddy used to give them to me, too." She blinked, and her eyes were instantly covered with a layer of tears that refused to fall. I thanked her and made my way through the crowd to my father's side.

I carefully placed the buckeye in his flannel pocket and let my hand rest upon the soft cloth above his still heart for a moment.

I whispered, "Keep it. It'll bring you good luck, Daddy," and I felt a great peace wash over me.

Today, like my father was so long ago, I, too, am a collector and keeper of buckeyes. Indeed, they are keepsakes to me. They grace the nooks and crannies of my everyday life, and when I randomly discover one, I roll it around in my hands and imagine the luck rubbing onto my fingertips.

When I hold one in my hand and squeeze, I am ten years old again, and my father stands before me with pockets filled with treasures and secrets he so willingly shares with me. Perhaps that's the true power of buckeyes—not the supposed luck associated with them, but the fact that these simple pieces from nature connect one generation to another. They connect me to my father—*forever*.

Amber Lanier Nagle is the curator of many keepsakes. She is freelance writer specializing in prescriptive nonfiction pieces. Her articles have appeared in Grit, Mother Earth News, Georgia Magazine, Chatter, Get Out Chattanooga, Savannah Magazine, *and many others. She is the author of an eBook,* Southern Exposure: A Few Random, Rambling Retrospective Pieces of My Life *and teaches memoir writing and freelancing workshops throughout Northwest Georgia for writers of all skill levels. Connect with Amber at www.AmberNagle.com.*

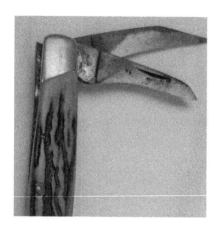

UNCLE JAMES' POCKET KNIFE

RENEA WINCHESTER

A memory keeper collects, gathers, plucks important items and hides them in safe places. Sometimes a memory keeper displays mementos for all to see. Sometimes memory keepers listen, hoard and stack-up stories waiting for the right moment to share them with anyone who shows a hint of interest.

This is a story about a knife.

My family observes Decoration Day. One day each spring, dozens of scattered family members travel to an area within the Great Smoky Mountains National Park to honor and remember our ancestors who once lived there. We help our children place flowers on *all* of the graves, because *all lives* matter.

"This is where you came from," we whisper to our young. "This is who you are." From the cemetery, we return to a park pavilion where those who are physically unable to make the ride and subsequent trek to the graves gather. Together, we enjoy a bounty of homemade goodies.

"Promise me you'll always do this," my uncle James said one year, referring to our family's Decoration Day ritual.

Uncle James had known—*even then*—that times were changing; that his nieces and nephews wouldn't care about their heritage as much as he did; that one day, people would forget; that one day tradition might die. It was the possibility of forgetting that worried him the most.

I had greeted him with a tiptoe kiss on the cheek, loving the feel of his stubbly cheek, inhaling the cigarette smoke which lingered on his skin. I loved how he bent down to accept my kiss even though I was an adult, both of us refusing to break our traditional greeting.

While he unfolded his body to his full height, I shook my head and responded, "Nope. I won't make that promise."

A frown lined his forehead. I suspect that among all of his relatives he hoped I would carry on the tradition.

"I won't promise, because to me, a promise is something that you might one day break," I said. "I won't promise because I've been coming to Decoration Day since I was a toddler. Nope. Don't worry about me one little bit. I'll always come, even if I'm the only one."

He seemed relieved.

Decades earlier our people had been displaced—moved, under duress, from their property called Indian Creek which is located on the North Carolina side of the National Park. James was the patriarch, the planner, the one who coordinated the gathering each year, and the one who made certain his relatives remembered. He was the family historian and story keeper.

When he wasn't working for the power company, he converted chunks of wood into beautiful creations. Using a simple pocketknife, he transformed wood into wonders doing so with an expertise I secretly longed to emulate. Back then, only boys were allowed to whittle. The same holds true today. There aren't many women carvers.

No one in the family could have anticipated my uncle's sudden death, or the enormous hole his home-going created.

During the spring of 2012, his daughter-in-law, Gail, honored his memory by attending Decoration Day. Instead of bringing a green bean casserole or a bucket of fried chicken, she brought a knife case filled with James' collection.

"I thought some of the nephews might like one of his knives," she announced.

As the boys gathered around, I whispered my request to her, "Can I pick one out?"

Peering into the red-velvet-lined case, I waited my turn as others selected new knives probably because they believed that the unopened boxes contained the more expensive tools.

"That's a good knife," one nephew said as the blade clicked into place.

"*Go ahead,*" I urged them secretly in my heart, "*Take your knives, just leave the one I want.*"

I waited my turn praying silently that the most valuable knife would remain when my turn came. With scratched silver edges and visible bits of rust, the knife I wanted had jingled with pocket change and been dumped on the dresser at the end of each tiring day. Bending my fingers around the tool, I slowly opened the blades. Testing each with my thumb, I struggled with my emotions. I could almost see James' fingers forcing the blade into a piece of cherry. The blades—worn slick with use—were, to me, perfect and priceless.

With a pierced heart and cascading tears, I closed the knife, pressed it to my heart then said in a trembling voice, "I'll take this one because it still bears his fingerprints. I want it because I remember him using it."

Gail could have sold his collection or donated the knives to a local charity. That's what people do these days, purge unwanted items from their life. For Gail to allow me the opportunity to carry James' knife is an incredible gift that I shall always treasure. I know she made him proud.

Later, after I told my mother of Gail's generosity she asked the question, "Which knife did you choose?"

Dad smiled and answered the question for me, "She chose well."

I carry the knife in my purse. Touching the dark grooves of the handle comforts me and gives me hope that family traditions will remain and that one day, I'll learn to carve just like my Uncle James.

Renea Winchester is the award-winning author of In the Garden with Billy: Lessons about Life, Love and Tomatoes, *a true-life tale of her experiences under the tutelage of a country farmer. She is also the author of* Stress-Free Marketing: Practical Advice for the Newly Published Author. *Her works have appeared in* Appalachian Heritage, Georgia Backroads, Smoky Mountain Living, Longleaf Style *and* Georgia Magazine. *She is a member of the Atlanta Writers Club, Georgia Writers Association, and the Roswell Garden Club. In 2012, the Atlanta Chapter of the National Association of Pen Women named her the Author of the Year. Connect with Renea at www.ReneaWinchester.com.*

MY BELOVED MIXING BOWL: "BIG GREEN"

MARCIA M. SWEARINGEN

Last night, as I prepared to make my husband's favorite meatloaf, I reached for *Big Green*. He was the largest in a graduated set of four bowls in varying shades of avocado green. The years have taken their toll. Now there are only two bowls, and now there are only two of us. But many cycles in the dishwasher and much fading have only enhanced the luster of my favorite bowl. We've been through a lot together, and I wouldn't think of a trade-in. Just to hold him in my arms brings back so many memories.

How could I forget the day we met—it was at my wedding shower. I received many gifts that day, but the beautifully wrapped package from my soon-to-be sister-in-law drew my

MY BELOVED MIXING BOWL: "BIG GREEN"

attention. Inside was something I knew I would use. Each colorful Pyrex bowl nested perfectly within its next larger neighbor. Maybe it was the meatloaf recipe she included—the one I still use—that spawned this memory. Meatloaf was the first call to duty for the virgin green bowl.

Like the mixing bowl, I was a rookie, too. No one ever told me that *"many cloves doth a bulb of garlic make."* My eyes still sting, my nose burns and I smile at the thought of my first meatloaf made with two *bulbs* of garlic and a pound of ground beef. Jim and I struggled with each bite—the new husband who couldn't speak a word of criticism and his bewildered wife without a clue. Money was so tight I froze the leftovers, but we never reheated them. Even the freezer stunk.

Another recipe from that same shower was for "No Fail Baked Alaska." Once again, *Big Green* sprang into action. Overnight in the freezer, he molded two layers of ice cream into an intriguing dome which I inverted onto a foil-covered baking sheet. The ice cream mountain went back in the freezer while I rinsed and readied *Big Green* for a massive beating of egg whites. Right before my eyes, copious mounds of frothy white foam threatened to overflow his edges. Soon I was icing my frozen masterpiece with mountains of meringue. I was so proud. The hard part was surrendering my trophy to a 400 degree gas oven so it could *brown*—something it never did. But the ice cream did what ice cream is prone to do under such circumstances—it became a Floating Alaska in the Honeymoon Hall of Fame.

With that kind of track record, *Big Green's* next role was more cosmetic than culinary. It was Halloween, and I didn't have a costume for a neighborhood party. Back in those days, roller derby was queen. In a flash of inspiration, I braided my hair, grabbed a green sports jersey, a pair of short shorts, my roller skates, and my crowning glory. *Big Green* became my helmet, secured by a couple of scarves looped over his spouts and tied under my neck.

When babies didn't come after three years of trying, my husband and I looked into adoption. Years of waiting finally culminated in a phone call late one Friday afternoon saying our child had been born, and we could pick her up at the hospital. Weighing only six pounds, she was dwarfed by our baby bathtub. Once again *Big Green* came to the rescue. I filled him with a quart of gently warmed water, and baby was a perfect fit.

As she grew, so did my cooking abilities. Over the years *Big Green* was the container of choice for mixing up batches of play dough, popsicles, trail mix, and homemade hot chocolate powder. His resume included friendship cakes, cornbread dressing, brownies, cookies, fruit cake, and four-bean salad. One Christmas he even helped with the preparation of divinity. I turned and scraped him as my hand mixer hummed, precariously suspended by its cord through the handle of an overhead cabinet above. The result was worth it—but only once.

Recently, I was cruising through the housewares section of Walmart when a colorful display caught my eye. It was a hot pink set of nesting plastic bowls, each with a large pour spout on one side and a smaller one on the other. For a moment, I thought how nice it would be to have a full set again. The price was not an obstacle, but I couldn't do it. Like the two people he's served for forty years, *Big Green* is not as pretty as he used to be—a little faded, but well-seasoned and comfortingly familiar to the touch.

Six years ago, he ably assisted me in making my daughter's favorite strawberry pudding recipe for a cookout two days before her wedding. The only part of her that still fits inside of him is her tasting finger. But now that she's expecting, I want a bowl with experience. And so the chronicles of *Big Green* continue.

MY BELOVED MIXING BOWL: "BIG GREEN"

Marcia Swearingen is a former newspaper editor and columnist specializing in inspirational nonfiction. Her stories have appeared in Guideposts *magazine and several Chicken Soup for the Soul and Cup of Comfort books. Her devotional columns have been published at www.MadetoMatter.org. She and her husband Jim enjoy golfing, gardening and about-to-be grand-parenting. They backyard bird-watch with a geriatric cat named Grace.*

BIRDIE B.'S SILVER SCISSORS

SHARON HUEY

I stood on the rocker of Mother's chair and looked over her shoulder as she did some hand sewing. I wanted to be outside, but a recent bout with pneumonia kept me tied to her apron strings. Mother showed the most compassion when I was sick, her tenderness boundless during those times. The healthier I became, the more the disciplinarian emerged in her. She wanted me off the rockers of her chair.

"Sharon, bring me my little scissors." I could hear the edgy pitch in her voice.

"Which ones are they?" I asked, hopping off the rocker. The chair lunged forward.

"The little scissors with the piece of red material on the handle," she heaved a sigh.

I found the scissors on the sewing machine and carried them to her bedroom where she sat in a chair listening to the TV but paying more attention to her needle and thread. She brought the thread to her front teeth and bit it off close to the material. The stringy leftovers she clipped away with the silver scissors.

"Why did you have to have *those* scissors?"

"They are the only ones that will do."

"But why?"

"Sharon, you make me tired."

I looked off into space hoping to let myself drift in a day dream when she said, "They belonged to my mama."

"They did?" I couldn't believe she ever had a mother. "Your mama?"

"Yes, your grandmother. She was an excellent seamstress. She made all my clothes. Once when I was in college, she made me a brown and yellow dress that was a perfect copy of the latest fashion. A girl in my dorm asked if she could borrow it. I didn't even share clothes with my sisters, but I let her wear the dress. The Dean of Women called me to her office and got on to me for loaning that darling dress that my mama had put so much work into. I got the dress back and never let anyone else wear my clothes again."

"Did my grandmother know me?"

"No, she died before you were born." Mother trimmed and snipped at wayward threads as she talked.

"These little scissors belonged to her. See this piece of fabric tied to the handle?"

"Yes."

"This is from the last dress she ever made before she died."

"Oh," I rubbed the frayed red cotton between my thumb and index finger. "Soft."

"She started me out sewing pillow cases with a simple over and under straight stitch. Soon, she had me making underwear and bed clothes."

"Underwear? You made underwear?"

"Yes, I did. Eventually, she taught me to sew on the machine. My baby brother, Bruce, would crawl under the sewing machine in the afternoon and take a nap. I guess the sounds of Mama and me talking combined with the machine going just put him right to sleep."

"Is he a grown up man, now?"

"Yes, you know him—Uncle Bruce."

"That's funny that he slept under the sewing machine."

"We all worked in the yard, the kitchen, or washing. Nobody was going to stop and put the baby down for a nap. He just slept wherever he was comfortable. He liked to get under Mama's machine."

"Did your sewing machine that you have now, belong to your mama?"

"Yes, after Mama died, your daddy and I brought her sewing machine home with us. Mama's machine was brand new, only a few months old. I was the only one of the girls interested in sewing, so I got her machine. When we got it home and set up, your daddy and I could not thread the bobbin. I wanted to use the machine so badly, but after weeks and weeks of trying, we still could not figure out how to make it work. It sat idle. Finally, I just gave up on sewing."

Mother paused and concentrated on her own stitches. I sat on the floor to get a better look at her face. Were her eyes misting behind her thick glasses?

"So what happened?" I prompted.

"I probably shouldn't tell you this. It will make you believe in ghosts or something."

"No, I won't. Please tell me." Mother considered whether to tell me the story or not. "Please," I said.

"Well, all right. One night about three weeks after she had died, Mama came to me in a dream." Mother looked and sounded excited. "She stood right in front of me and said: *"Birdie, this is how you do it."* She held the bobbin in one hand and the case in the other."

Mother's voice took on a mystical quality, soft and full of awe. She blinked away several tears but continued.

"Mama clicked the bobbin into its case, pulled and tightened the thread just so with her fingers, and dropped the bobbin in the machine. She showed me with her own hands. When I woke up in the morning, I felt wonderful because I had been with Mama. I went straight to the machine and threaded the bobbin. That was in 1940 before you were born. I still miss her." Mother wiped at her eyes. "Sharon, get me a Kleenex."

I pulled a Kleenex out of the box on the dresser and handed it to her. She dabbed at her eyes.

"Mama used to say, 'Work is our salvation.'"

"What did she mean by that?"

"She meant if a person is busy, they don't have to dwell on things so much."

"What things?"

"Back then, children died of pneumonia, diphtheria, and typhoid. We didn't have booster shots."

"Died?" I had only heard of one child dying, and she had fallen from a high tree limb.

"Yes, back then life was hard. Only four of Mama's nine children lived to be adults."

I quieted thinking about my recent run-in with pneumonia, while Mother pushed forward quickly with her story.

"I asked Mama once which one was the hardest to lose. That was after my older brother Orrin died. He was only forty years old when he died of cancer." Mother shook her head. "Mama said, 'Well, the longer you have a child, of course, the more you love it, but the one I grieve over most is the baby.'"

Mother circled the thread around her finger and pulled until a knot appeared. Using the scissors she cut a dangling piece of thread close to the loop. She continued the story.

"Papa went to L.S.U. in the summer of 1912 to start his master's degree. The board of education had said that all principals had to have their masters, or they could not stay in the job. Papa rode a horse to Baton Rouge, which took several weeks. When the ten-month old baby got very sick, Mama had no way to reach Papa."

"Weren't there any phones?"

"Yes, but not along the way. Papa stayed in farmers' barns or camped out in the open while he traveled. Mama sent a telegram to L.S.U. By the time he received the message that there was trouble at home, the baby had died and been buried. He grieved so much over the loss of the baby and not being at home when Mama needed him that he told the school board he didn't want to be principal anymore. That is how he became the postmaster."

Mother bit off another thread and sliced it close to the edge of the material with the silver scissors.

"What did the baby die of?"

"I don't know—probably pneumonia or flu. A lot of babies died back then."

"Oh." I thought about that for a minute. "Would that baby have been your brother or sister?"

"My baby sister, yes. Here, put my little scissors back. Be careful. They are sharp."

I carried the little scissors with the red material still dangling from the handle back to the sewing box. They felt like nothing in my hand, but in my heart they placed me back in a time where I saw and heard the secrets of a strong, brave woman, a grandmother I never knew.

Just as my mother and grandmother sewed using the little silver scissors, so do I. The faded red cloth, a remnant of the last dress my grandmother sewed over seventy years ago, remains tied to the handle of my little scissors even as I use them today, binding me spiritually to place, people, tradition, and stories that have to be told.

As an English and Drama teacher, Sharon Huey sponsored literary magazines, directed plays, and coached individual speaking events and mock trials before retiring in front of the computer screen with a blank mind. She is looking for representation for her first novel, Listen to the Lambs, *and is working on a second novel.*

MY FATHER'S FOUNTAIN PEN

ESTELLE RODIS-BROWN

My father was an old man with an ancient soul—even when he was young. He was a fountain pen among ballpoints, and he was proud to stand by the old, outdated ways that seemed laughable to trendy folks. It's no surprise then, after he passed away at the age of nearly ninety-one, that I found an amber-handled Regal fountain pen with an all-but-used bottle of ink inside one of his desks.

I keep this gold-tipped pen at my desk now to remind me of dear old Dad. Even though I'm writing on a computer keyboard, I draw inspiration simply by gazing at this elegant writing implement, and comfort in knowing that my father continues to guide me, even from the *Great Beyond*.

On occasion, I dip this pen back into its inkwell, just as my father may have done to write Army Intelligence reports in Nazi-occupied Germany during World War II; then later to craft love letters to my mother; then as a history instructor to American GIs in France and Italy. After earning his Ph.D. and throughout his career, he used it to grade the papers of his college history students, or to scrawl out the worries and prayers that often kept him awake at night.

Always professorial, he played the part of the tweedy old gentleman in a bow tie and woolen driver's cap—only he wasn't play-acting. He was the genuine article. And he continued to use fountain pens and manual typewriters long after ballpoints and personal computers had overtaken the modern world.

In 1917, Themistocles Constantine Rodopoulos (our family name was changed to 'Rodis' by U.S. immigration officials) became the firstborn son to barely educated Greek peasants who had immigrated to America in hopes of a better life for their children. His big name seemed to bear the big dreams of his parents.

Although my father didn't even start school until he was eight years old (simply because his folks didn't realize he was supposed to be there), he loved to learn and soon mastered English, becoming a star pupil and a voracious reader.

Life was hard for the new Americans. The Great Depression and a growing family kept them in a state of poverty. But they were steadfast believers that hard work, firm morals and a good education could elevate them to a respectful status. Dad's father lived the American Dream by working up from a shoeshine boy to an independent business owner.

"You can do anything you set your mind to, as long as you're willing to work hard and stick with it," my father liked to say.

He proved it by working full time at his father's (and uncle's) sandwich shop, Peter's Cafe in downtown Cleveland, while earning his bachelor's and master's degrees. When he considered a law degree at George Washington University in D.C., he worked full time for the U.S. Treasury and as an assistant professor at University of Maryland.

A member of the Greatest Generation, he served in the Army during the war. Although he was exempt from the draft because he was supporting his family due to his father's losing battle with stomach cancer, he volunteered because he was driven by principle. It was the right and honorable thing to do. That's the impulse that drove my father throughout his long life.

He was more a thinker than a doer, sharing the wisdom of philosophers, saints and sages with those around him. He had a maxim or two for every occasion. "Better look before you leap," he'd warn me, whenever I contemplated something new. Always trying to moderate my characteristic impatience and impulsivity, he'd often advise, "Don't bite off more than you can chew. Rome wasn't built in a day, you know."

Dad ruled the house by The Law of Rodis, which was his particular set of moral absolutes he expected us five kids to abide by. Chief among them: Benjamin Franklin's "Honesty is the best policy;" "Waste not, want not;" "Early to bed and early to rise makes a man healthy, wealthy and wise;" and "Save that for a rainy day."

My father valued the process as much as the result, which may explain his penchant for fountain pens. He felt that one's work was a reflection of one's character, so "The only job worth doing is a job well done."

It was just like Dad to complicate something simple (like writing) that it may drive home any lessons that could be learned. If you've ever used an old-fashioned fountain pen (not the new-fangled kind with a disposable ink cartridge), you know it can be a clumsy tool for beginners. If you get too much ink on the tip, you'll blemish the page with a ruinous dark blob that drowns out surrounding script. If you fail to get enough ink on the tip, you'll stutter-start your attempt to write, probably ripping paper in the effort to drag the dry stylus across the page.

It takes patience and a learned rhythm to write successfully and gracefully with a fountain pen. Once you've mastered it, there's no smoother experience in writing. It's fluid and beautiful, like a precious, special occasion.

Thanks to his devotion to the Greek Orthodox Church, my father liked to turn everyday activities into religious rites. It transformed every meal, every graded paper, every research project into a mini-liturgy. His fountain pen was like a holy censor, infusing each task with prayerful incense.

I've always loved and respected my father, but he was not easy on us. His expectations were unrealistically high. Whenever we brought home a meritorious report card, he'd tell the story about how he finally brought home all A's and his father simply retorted, "Why didn't you do that before?" So much for a pat on the back.

As I came of age, the Cat Stevens hit, *Father and Son*, became my signature song. The father says, "It's not time to make a change. Just relax, take it easy. You're still young. That's your fault. There's so much you have to know . . ." The son replies, "From the moment I could talk, I was ordered to listen. Now there's a way and I know, that I have to go away."

I may not have been a son, but I was in a painful struggle with my father. I felt he was full of contradictions ("Do as I say; not as I do"), stuck in the past, disengaged from reality. He wanted me to slow down, stay close to home, learn from his experiences. In stark contrast, I craved to break away, hit the road, discover new things and learn from my own experiences.

Dad disowned me when I was nineteen, after I announced I was taking a cross-country trek with my boyfriend so we could work a summer job in Washington State. Along the way, we became engaged. My fiancée never asked his future father-in-law for his daughter's hand in marriage. My dad's world was falling apart. He was like Reb Tevye in *Fiddler on the Roof*. How could his youngest daughter thumb her nose at sacred tradition?

It took time, but we eventually began talking again. Dad ultimately reinstated me as his daughter, but he never gave up ground. I responded in kind. We allowed love to cover all wounds, and built from there. The ink of love flowed between us once again. Through the years, I would find scraps of paper tucked into my backpack, purse or baby bag, bearing the illegible longhand of my father offering advice, support, encouragement—*his love*.

And now, four years since his passing, Dad remains very much alive. Why? Partly because he left behind rooms full of books, papers, photographs, newspaper clippings and notes that serve as a continuing conversation about what intrigued, beguiled and concerned him.

As well, his incessant repetition of the tenets of The Law of Rodis did their work in me. Now, every time one of my children comes to me with a pressing issue, I find myself repeating Dad's words: "There's a time and a place for everything, honey. Just be patient and everything will work out for the best." Or, "Where there's a will, there's a way. Just don't give up and you're bound to succeed."

And when I miss Dad most, I pick up his old fountain pen, dip it in its inkwell and write his name in strong, fluid strokes: Themistocles Constantine Rodopoulos. Rest in peace until we meet again, Dad, because as you always said, "It's never goodbye; just so long for now."

MY FATHER'S FOUNTAIN PEN

Estelle Rodis-Brown is a freelance writer and public relations specialist who inherited a love of history and collecting keepsakes from her father, and the love of aesthetics and neatness from her mother. This inner tension makes for a life of perfect balance (hah!). Estelle also enjoys creating photography and stoneware pottery, traveling, gardening, and bicycling. She and her husband, Foster, live in northeast Ohio with their three children and their beloved mutt, Sugar.

THE PREGNANCY SHIRT

COLEEN BROOKS

It's not a fancy shirt, but I wore it throughout all four of my pregnancies. My mother-in-law and her sister bought it at a yard sale down in Florida sometime in 1972. When they first spotted the carefully folded shirt, it immediately struck their fancy, and the price was right at seventy-five cents, so they bought it.

Even the coloring is nondescript. It's kind of a light brown but not quite tan, with big pockets and pale green embroidered Native American designs on the back and along the zippered V-neck. It's obviously homemade and just *hippie* enough for me to love it.

Marriage came to me one year after college to a young man with black curls and equally black eyes. He had a killer smile with even white teeth. He didn't ride up to my castle (which was a blue and white trailer at the time) on a white stallion, but he did drive a white Corvette. That car, by itself, was enough to get me interested.

After a short, whirlwind romance, we married causing tongues to wag in our small Southern town. Most of the society ladies surmised that the only reason a young couple married so quickly was because a "bun was in the oven."

My husband and I fooled a lot of folks.

Because we were considered older for marriage back in those days at twenty-three and twenty-seven respectively, we wanted children quickly, and we wanted a large family. Not being able to conceive *never* entered my mind. I figured within a few months into the marriage, we'd be anxiously awaiting the birth of our first child.

But that didn't happen.

After a year of disappointment, we started going to specialists. I took fertility pills, and tests were run on both of us. I still smile when I think of my darling young husband having to provide a specimen to be analyzed.

"Well, that's the least romantic thing I have ever done," he announced to me in the specimen lab.

We did a lot of unromantic things during that time, but four years passed with no pregnancy—no child. As we began to consider adoption, a last ditch effort was offered to me. I could have exploratory surgery. Without a moment's hesitation, I agreed, and the surgery was performed. One month later, we were expecting.

During the years preceding my miraculous, fertility surgery, we learned a tough lesson—that people are at times, thoughtless and insensitive.

"You sure have been married a long time," some of our friends and acquaintances would say. "When are you going to start a family?"

"Oh, we are going to wait a while before we have children," I would reply, trying to be upbeat as I choked back tears.

"Well, you better not wait too long, or it may be too late," they would note.

It hurt to be constantly reminded of our childlessness, when we so desperately wanted a baby.

But my mother-in-law understood. Sometimes she was with me when someone asked the inevitable question.

"You will have children someday—I just know it," she reassured me in that sweet South Alabama drawl.

And this is what the pregnancy shirt is all about.

My mother-in-law—I called her, Mother—knew I'd be crazy about it. She kept it hidden away just waiting for the right moment to present it to me.

"It just looked like you," she said as I eagerly tried it on one day. "Perfect—just a perfect fit."

I never got really huge with any of my pregnancies, so the little shirt fit me well all the way up to the delivery. In fact, I wore it to the hospital the day our first child came into this world—a beautiful baby daughter we named, Heather.

For each of the other pregnancies, the shirt came out of storage. The only time I thought the shirt might not fit was in my ninth month of pregnancy number two. I had mad cravings for Peppermint Patties and gained around forty pounds. The shirt just barely covered my oversized belly, but it *did*, and that is what was important.

I wore that shirt to the hospital for each of the births. I'm not normally superstitious, but I felt the need to wear it. Somehow, I knew that if I wore the pregnancy shirt, everything would be all right.

I never wore the shirt any other time except during pregnancy. Four children completed our family. At almost thirty-six,

THE PREGNANCY SHIRT

I decided, although the decision wasn't easy, that my pregnancy years were over. It seemed like I'd been constantly pregnant from 1973 to 1983. The shirt was no longer needed, and it became a keepsake.

As the years sped by and our children grew up, I didn't even think about the little shirt, not until my daughter told me she was pregnant with her first child. I knew that Heather loved the shirt also, and we had even talked about my giving it to her when she *did* become pregnant.

It had been years since I had seen the shirt. I thought I had put it in an old blue trunk where I stored some other keepsakes, but when I went to fetch it, it wasn't there. Searching high and low, it was nowhere to be found. I was devastated. The shirt had been so special to me. I had visions of it accidentally being put in with clothes donated to the Salvation Army or some other charitable place. Where could it be, and how could I be so careless with something so precious, even if it was just a plain old homemade shirt?

Heather never got to wear the shirt for either of her pregnancies, and I figured the shirt was lost forever. I gained some comfort in the fact that maybe someone—somewhere—wore it for her first pregnancy.

But other times, reality would reign. I knew that the shirt was really old, that the pocket needed to be repaired and a tear in the side stitching needed to be mended. Deep inside, I knew that nobody would want the timeworn, out-of-style garment. Only my daughter and I cared about that shirt. We looked at it as *vintage*, but no one else would. I thought in horror, that it probably ended up being used as a rag.

One day, as my second born son was rummaging around in boxes up in the attic, he came into the living room, and in his hands, he held the little pregnancy shirt.

"Haven't you been looking for this, Mom?" he asked. "I remember you wearing it when you were pregnant with Hartwell."

The shirt had somehow been put in a box and shoved into the attic. When he gave it to me, I cried. Examining it, I found no moth holes. Nothing had hurt it. It was still in the same shape as before—worn, but wearable.

I don't know why I love the shirt so much. Maybe it's because of the spacious pockets. Maybe it's because it's just so soft and comfortable. But most of all, I think it's because my mother-in-law and her sister, my dear Aunt Rosie, picked it out especially for me. They didn't really know at the time that I would ever get pregnant, but they were *hopeful*.

The pregnancy shirt, once lost, but now found, is kept in a special place in a drawer in my dresser. I haven't repaired the pocket or the hole yet. No matter. I pull it out every so often and just hold it to my face. I can almost smell the *baby magic* it once rubbed on my pregnant belly. It makes me smile.

My oldest son and his wife are trying to have a baby. They are having problems getting pregnant. I understand their pain. So the little shirt waits in the drawer, and I am *hopeful*.

Coleen Brooks is a longtime resident of Cahoun, Georgia and has been educator off and on for over forty years. She is currently the Assistant Director of Adult Education for Georgia Northwestern Technical College. A writer all of her life, Coleen now writes for Calhoun Magazine, *entertains friends with her blog, www.litlmarysunshine.blogspot.com, and is involved in the Calhoun Little Theatre as an actress and director.*

THE EASTMAN CHEMICAL TANK CAR

PAUL GARRISON

I cannot imagine being born into better circumstances. I was born a healthy, white male in 1963 in Austin, Texas. The birth control pill was not widely used. Abortion was illegal. Major diseases had been tamed. I had loving parents, a big sister, a nice house, warm clothes, good food, a bedroom of my own, and plenty of toys. I could play every day and not worry about a thing. My favorite toy was a Lionel train set.

The trains were not really *my* toy trains—they were my father's. The train set came out only once a year, for about a month around Christmas. My father, Lawrence Garrison, pulled out the boxes and assembled all the pieces into electro-mechanical magnificence. There were straight tracks, curved tracks, criss-crossed tracks, tracks with turnouts, a diesel locomotive, freight cars, chemical cars, a caboose, an engineer, and a controller I used to talk to the engineer. I remember the train cars and track as being big—much bigger than the little model train sets you see today. I don't know if they were really that big or if I was small and everything just *seemed* big. They had lots of detail, as if perfectly shrunken from real freight trains, complete with decals, hand rails, steps, doors, and steel wheels. All the parts which *should* move, *did* move. The set was not immense nor did it have every possible accessory. Quite a lot was left to my imagination. It fit on one or two pieces of plywood.

I watched the train for hours as it stopped and started and looped and ran figure eights. I loaded the freight cars with cargo, filled the chemical cars with liquid and delivered the load to the other side of the track. My father held my hands as I directed the engineer to turn or stop. From then on, I was destined to be an engineer.

But I almost didn't get to play with the trains. At six days old, I was adopted by my mother and father—Margaret and Lawrence Garrison. I never saw my birth mother again. She was Catholic, unwed, and a teenager. I have been told her family sent her out of state to have me and put me up for adoption. The Catholic Dioceses of Austin housed her, made sure she had medical care, and found a good family for me. A priest at the Dioceses, who I would come to know as Uncle Georgy, played a major role in finding families for infants.

Uncle Georgy carried significant influence at the Dioceses. Two years earlier, he helped my parents—a childless, well educated, Catholic couple—adopt a baby girl on very short notice. They were overjoyed and named her "Georgia," after him. Uncle Georgy also made sure the couple adopted me, and so I became the *baby* of the Garrison family.

THE EASTMAN CHEMICAL TANK CAR

Uncle Georgy was very fond of my Mom and made routine visits to our house. He came over frequently for lunch or dinner and was part of our extended family. He loved photography. Indeed, the best pictures of our family were taken by Uncle Georgy—one of my mom in her high back chair smoking a cigarette, one of the family and Uncle Georgy at the dinner table, one of me marching, playing my red drum through the living room, and one of Georgia sitting on the trunk of a fallen oak tree. The focus, composition, and lighting of these photos are fabulous, as if Ansel Adams had taken and developed them himself.

Mom was an only child, and her parents had died before I was born, so I had no aunts or uncles or grandparents on my mother's side. This did not concern me, though, because I had an abundance of relatives on my father's side. There was Shady Grandma, named for small farm she had in Shady, New York. I had Uncle Charlie, Aunt Sally, and Aunt Gloria and a gaggle of cousins. We visited them each summer. We pulled up, and the entire family poured out of the house, hugging and kissing each of us. I even had to hug and kiss wrinkled Shady Grandma, who smelled like an old leather shoe, but that was okay because we *belonged* and were home.

I was the baby among the cousins, too, and everyone kept an eye on me. We played hide and seek in Shady Grandma's corn fields, climbed her huge, old trees, and then went to Uncle Charlie's house to swim in the pool. I could not swim at all. I could only doggy paddle and grab any passing cousin for safety. The adults talked, sipped their drinks, and yelled at us not to run around the pool. We ate hot dogs and hamburgers, and at night, the boys piled into one room to sleep.

Back in Texas, my sister, Georgia, was my constant companion, playmate, and overseer. One day, I "went to work" on the back patio, riding my red, Radio Flyer tricycle while Georgia played across the concrete, doing some girl thing in which I had no interest. I noticed something on the house that needed repair. Fortunately, I had my tools handy, including my screwdriver. I rode over to investigate. Sure enough, there were holes in the house, tiny little slots just big enough for my screwdriver. I stuck the screwdriver into a slot. Sparks flew out of the slot, and it felt as if one hundred yellow jackets had stung my hand. First I screamed, and then I wailed and wailed and wailed. My hand had burns, but I was okay. Afterwards, Georgia got in big trouble. Apparently, at six, she was supposed to be supervising me.

Then in the fall of 1968, my father woke my sister and I very early one morning to see Apollo 5 fly overhead. With no lights on, we went into the dark front yard and looked up at the sky which sparkled with stars. Within a few minutes, one very bright star appeared on the horizon moving quickly, silently, across the sky. It was the spaceship that would take a man to the moon.

The following Christmas, I, too, joined the mission and deployed the toy trains to the moon and back—*in my imagination.*

On a cool, clear spring day before my fifth birthday, those toy trains had a terrible crash, spilling the freight and liquid chemicals all over my life and wreaking havoc. As my father and I tossed a football in the front yard, Mom and Uncle Georgy drove up in a new blue Chevy Bel Air. They parked at the curb, which was odd. I soon learned that my mom had divorced my father and married the priest—Uncle Georgy. They were moving to Missouri and had come to get me and my sister, and take us far away from the father and the life we loved.

The trip was rough for me. I got motion sick very easily. Right after we departed, I complained about feeling like I had

THE EASTMAN CHEMICAL TANK CAR

to throw-up. The feeling continued to get worse and worse, and I complained more. Uncle Georgy pulled off the highway. I got out of the car, walked around for a few minutes, and quickly felt all better. So we loaded the car and off we went again. Just as quickly as I became well, I started feeling sick all over again. Uncle Georgy pulled off again. This went on several times, stopping and starting, inching along, until somewhere in north Texas, Uncle Georgy had enough and told me to just get sick out of the back window—and I did. I spewed my lunch and bile all over the back quarter panel of the new car. This release cured me.

By the time we were Oklahoma, I regained enough strength to start my revolt. I figured out I did not want any part of the move and became a first-class brat. Uncle Georgy could take no more, pulled over once again, and gave me my first spanking. I cried, and my nose ran. I think this is where he decided to change my given name to *Snot*, a name that he, *and only he*, called me for the next twenty years.

Life rolled along in a different direction. After my parents divorced, my father, Lawrence, married another woman, and Georgia and I spent the next few summers visiting him and his new wife. But we never visited around Christmas, so I never saw the trains. We didn't have any of our other toys to play with either. Instead, we passed the time trying to throw a golf ball into the cup on a putting green, feeding the tame squirrels at the apartment complex, and refinishing old wooden furniture.

As a consolation for not playing with the trains, my father gave me a new model train tank car from his work, the Eastman Chemical Company. It was a single chemical car glued to a single piece of track. It was much smaller than Dad's real toy trains, but like them, it had a lot of detail. It had the Eastman

Chemical Products decal, had valves and ladders, and could carry 60,000 pounds, but it did not move and had no moving parts, and it was no substitute. I kept the mounted tank car in my summertime room and imagined filling it with water for the next Apollo mission to the moon. We continued our summer visits and even saw our Shady family from time to time.

On Halloween, when I was ten, Georgia and I made our neighborhood rounds and were flush with candy. I was sucking every bit of flavor out a piece of butterscotch candy, which was my favorite candy, when the phone rang. Mom answered the mustard-colored, rotary phone hanging on the kitchen wall. The pleasant look on her face drained at once. She turned her back to us and lowered her voice, asking questions. Georgia and I stopped everything and focused totally on her, trying to learn the secret. After a minute, she hung up and turned to us.

"Your father had a massive heart attack," Mom said. "He was waiting for a commuter train in Philadelphia this morning, and he had a heart attack."

We stood there, silent and stunned.

"They tried to revive him, but they couldn't," she continued. "He died."

I spit out my butterscotch candy and cried.

Over the next few days Georgia and I waited for more details. The next day came and went. We never heard from my father's new wife. We never heard from Uncle Charlie, Aunt Sally, or Aunt Gloria. We were never told about funeral arrangements. We didn't go to the Wake, the Requiem Mass, or the burial. For us, one day just went on to the next, as if nothing happened.

A few weeks later, I asked about my father's belongings. In my mind, I thought they should be given to me and Georgia. I wanted the train set and my father's coin collection.

My Mom called the new wife and made my request. A month later, a small box arrived with the coins and a few other things, but no train set. The trains were gone. And the Shady family was gone, too. Georgia and I never got a call or card from them again. That part of my family had been severed—*amputated*. The train track abruptly ended then and there, with the death of my father.

Each new day brought new tracks and new destinations. Uncle Georgy provided for me and Georgia, making sure we had life's necessities and doing his best to make us decent, well-adjusted people. We eventually called him *Dad*, and he became our dad, though to him, I was still, *Snot*.

Over the next thirty-six years, I experienced mostly great fortune. I did not get drafted into war. I graduated from Georgia Tech, met my beautiful wife, Annie, and found excellent work. Annie and I travelled the world and participated in the Internet boom. I lived a life most would envy.

Then in 2009, Uncle Georgy's—Dad's—health declined dramatically. He developed what he called a serious case of the *don't give a shits*. For years, he had been the main caregiver for my mother, who lived with dementia and stayed in bed all day, every day. He lost a lot of weight and was not too concerned about any of it.

He died in May that year. I had seen it coming and was as prepared as I could be. I told my mom, but she never fully digested the news. Georgia and I found a funeral home and scheduled the cremation, just as Dad requested. He had asked us to plan the least expensive funeral possible, and we obliged. We bought an inexpensive, marble urn for his ashes.

We started planning a visitation, funeral, and burial. We called Dad's family in California. They had not seen or spoken to him in years. They were saddened but would not, or could not, come. We called Dad's work to see who might come, and the next day, got a call back saying there was no interest. Our family had stopped attending church years before, so there was no congregation to offer support. Only the next door neighbors expressed feigning interest, just trying to be polite.

Funerals are for the living, and it seemed Georgia, Annie, and I were the only ones who cared. In reality, funerals are not necessary—a lesson Georgia and I learned almost forty years before. And so, we had no funeral.

Georgia and I found a nursing home for Mom and made sure she was comfortable and as well-cared for, as possible. We spent months going to my parents' house, cleaning, and going through the hoards of belongings. In boxes in the attic, we found Dad's Rollieflex camera and all the pictures of our family from Texas. We also found the Eastman Chemical tank car, still glued to its single track. It must have been in that small box delivered to our house thirty-six years ago, when I was denied the real toy train set. I took it home and placed it on our fireplace mantel, so I could see it.

A ten-year-old boy nor a forty-eight-year-old man never fully recovers from the divorce of his parents and the death his father—or, fathers. Those wounds had scarred over and life had moved on, but Annie knew I still had a hole where my Shady family existed. She knew it still hurt.

And so, Annie found and contacted Uncle Charlie and some of the members of the Shady family. Charlie was delighted to hear from her and to hear Georgia and I were doing well. He wanted to talk to us, to see us, for us to come to New Jersey and visit the Garrison clan.

I spoke to Uncle Charlie several times over the next few months and learned the answers to many of my questions.

"Was there a funeral?" I asked.

THE EASTMAN CHEMICAL TANK CAR

"Yes," Charlie answered. "The entire family, except you and Georgia, attended the gathering, and only the new wife's family went to the funeral in Texas."

"Were there pictures of my father?" I asked.

There were lots of family pictures, and Uncle Charlie graciously sent copies to me.

"Georgia and I got very little of my father's belongings after he died," I said to Charlie one day on the phone. "The thing I wanted most was the train set."

My uncle paused for a moment and said in a subdued tone, "Paul, I know where the trains are. We got them back. They had been in our family long before Lawrence had them."

As he spoke, I held a fleeting hope that he was about to offer to send them to me, but he didn't.

For months, Uncle Charlie tried to reestablish a relationship with me, but I could not reciprocate. To me, that track ended years ago, and trying to rebuild it now could never make it whole again, or make up for lost time.

I am now content imagining that one of my cousins continues the tradition—pulling the train set out every Christmas, building the pieces into electromechanical magnificence and letting one of his children take it to the moon and back.

Mom's good physical health continues to surprise me, as her dementia slowly worsens. She sits and waits for visitors from the other side—her father, the Fair Edith (her step mother) or from George, the high Catholic priest adorned in his glorious regalia. Dad sits in his marble urn on a shelf in my sister's spare bedroom, waiting for Mom to join him. And the Eastman Chemical tank car sits on my mantel, empty and fastened to its track, waiting for me, as the rest of my beautiful life whooshes by on other tracks.

PAUL GARRISON

Paul Garrison works for an insurance services company. He and Annie live out in the middle of nowhere with three big dogs. He works and rides his bike up and down country roads. He visited his mother every weekend until her death in September 2012.

THE CUSTARD SPOON

JEAN LOWREY

The spoon is worn. What wouldn't be after seventy years of use? The cream-colored, nylon pot-stirring tool is also browned a bit in the concave scoop and melted somewhat at the tip. Long ago, before plastic was recycled, it would have found itself in a landfill or at least in a second-hand or maybe even third-hand shop had it not been for its true calling.

Yes, it stirred green beans and fatback that were boiled within an inch of burning. It whipped creamed potatoes and then baptized them—dunking, not sprinkling—with a gob of butter and a shower of salt. It magically mixed drippings, flour and milk into succulent gravy to drizzle on biscuits, chicken, or beef.

Wistfully, I held that spoon in my hand in January 1991 as my four siblings and I divided our grandmother's treasures.

Throughout her apartment were big and small keepsakes: her hand-painted china always with gold rims, her meticulously crocheted sweaters and blankets, her lifelike drawings and paintings artfully composed in a style expected of an early 20th century young lady.

Her Brownie Kodak camera's big square slides took us on vicarious visits to all forty-eight contiguous states plus Hawaii while her hand-written vacation diaries beckoned our fantasies to other alluring destinations. Her plentiful postcards mailed from all over America. told stories of the traveling-salesman grandfather we never knew.

A later-in-life conversion from homemaker to elementary school teacher and from mother to grandmother transformed her personal book collection as well. Her library, scattered decoratively on bookshelves and tables throughout her apartment, transported us to encounters with Nostradamus or adventures with "Cubby in Wonderland."

The big Curtis Mathes television, whose once seemingly huge twenty-five-inch screen brought us together to watch the annual Macy's Thanksgiving Day Parade, sat in the next room unclaimed. My grandfather's solid wood, knee-hole desk and ladder-back chair, comprising an early 20th century salesman's work station, awaited a taker. So did beds, sofas, tables, chairs, footstools, bookshelves, cabinets, lamps, linen and dishes.

A closet-full of "smart" coat-dresses, regular dresses, skirts, blouses, pants, shoes and sandals stood as testimony to her widely-admired gift of style. It was a fashion array that spoke of church, bridge parties, cross-country travels and beach vacations.

So why was I holding the tired spoon, the kind you put out-of-sight when company comes? Twisting it, I imagined how and when the discoloration and melting had occurred. Then, I pictured the bounteous menus wrought from its work. I heard silverware clink upon china and tinkle in crystal. Finally, I saw familiar family and friends—each fed by this spoon.

I saw a wrinkled, aged-spotted hand slowly and gently guiding the spoon, around and around and around the pot as a cream-colored recipe continued to thicken and coat the sides of the pot and the spoon. Around and around, again and again. Thickening and coating. Mesmerizing motions. The hand and the spoon working as one.

Around and around, she continued to stir. With her free hand, she swatted at a fly which had located the lone hole in the kitchen window screen.

With that same free hand, she dabbed at the salty dew that materialized on her forehead and trickled downward, burning her eyes. That old window fan down the hall couldn't do much about the Georgia humidity or heat. Around and around. The thin, cottonprint house-dress would sway breezily if only a zephyr could be summoned. Again and again. Thickening and coating.

Finally, the hand and the spoon stopped their revolutions. Sweet boiled custard—the sugar, flour, eggs, milk and vanilla blended to perfection by the spoon—was ready to remove from the heat. A quick tap of the spoon against the pot rim sent custard snuggled into the spoon's bowl back into the pot. After she gave the spoon a quick lick, which she justified as *quality control*, she tossed the spoon into sudsy dishwater. She hugged the dutch oven with potholders to move it from the hot stove eye to an unlit one. For the hopeful grandchildren, the wait until the custard was cool enough to eat seemed interminable.

That hand and that spoon collaborated on many occasions to welcome a new baby into the world, to wish a happy birthday, to greet an old or new acquaintance, to nourish a sick friend, to support those grieving, to provide a favorite dessert or to create a memory.

My husband bonded with my grandmother over her boiled custard. Though not the only one to enjoy it, he convinced her that he was her number-one boiled custard fan. She responded often by making a batch just for him. The final message she left on our answering machine in November 1990 told Dick she had fresh boiled custard ready for him to pick up. Like other occasions, this trip resulted in Dick picking up not only the custard, but also the cook. And once again, she joined us for dinner where she entertained, listened to, consoled, counseled, laughed with and loved us.

The spoon, now christened *"The Custard Spoon,"* rests in my kitchen drawer. Occasionally, but really not often enough, it comes out to perform an old ritual. I stand over the stove and watch The Custard Spoon and my grandmother's hand as they collaborate once again to do a seemingly little thing—make boiled custard—to accomplish a much bigger thing—love and bless others. They stop stirring occasionally to check the thickness of the custard so that it is just right.

When they are finished, I know it is my duty, my privilege and my pleasure to share the custard with other people—but only after I follow my grandmother's quality control measure and lick The Custard Spoon.

Jean Lowrey retired from salaried jobs as Dalton Public Schools (Dalton, Georgia) public relations director and as Dalton Education Foundation executive director in 2011. She currently is a freelance writer whose work has been published in magazines, newspapers, web sites and other venues.

HARRY AFT'S SIGNET RING

DAVID AFT

Several years ago my father's father died. Shortly thereafter, the family decided to move my grandmother from the home she and my grandfather shared to a nursing home closer to my Uncle Larry's house outside of Atlanta. By the time his passing fully registered with Grandmother, she had lost much of herself to the ravages of old age, and as a consequence, so much of our collective memories of their lives was reduced to fragments—alive only in *our* minds.

The move set in motion a chain of events that involved the sifting through of the artifacts they had accumulated in their lifetime together. As the oldest son, the responsibility of tidying-up the family home fell by default to my father, and he and my mother began the arduous task of finding the true keepsakes amidst the trappings and trivia of my grandparents' lives. The process of going through everything took the better part of two weeks and presented numerous challenges.

I think my folks did a pretty good job identifying pieces that struck a chord with each son and grandchild. I don't recall hearing of any disputes arising out of the decision to give one uncle a souvenir from Grandpa and Grandma's trip to the Holy Land in 1974 or who ended-up with the candy dish that adorned my grandmother's coffee table for forty years. I know that no one wanted the seven cases of Safeguard soap that my mother discovered stashed in the linen closet, although the discovery added a moment of comic respite to an otherwise difficult and emotional task.

It is amazing what we collect during our lives. I expect each of us will leave a similarly onerous burden to our heirs as they decide what mattered and what merely served.

My dad and his father never really understood one another. Over the years, this disconnect did not get in the way of our holidays together or the many weddings and social gatherings that keep families connected. It really wasn't until I got older and watched their careful dance of tolerance and loyalty give way to frustration and indifference that I began to understand the depth of their disconnect. I think my dad always hoped that his father would understand him as a man—not as a grown child. And perhaps my grandfather always hoped that his oldest son would acknowledge and share his view of the world, which never happened either. Much to my father's credit, he never let these challenges pollute my relationship with Grandpa.

The strain, which always existed as an undertow, presented a few challenges to my father as he tried to see each relationship between father and son, or grandfather and grandson through the eyes of his father. I think their estrangement forced him to think with his head more than his heart and, as a result, the items he chose for each surviving son and grandson reflected what he thought would perpetuate our memories, forging a link to my grandfather and our individual recollections of him.

When every last item in their home had been dispatched to its next destination, my parents visited my brothers and me to deliver our keepsakes. In my case, they had chosen a sterling silver signet ring, etched with my grandfather's initials. The ring is simple and elegant, far different from my memories of Grandpa Harry, whose 6 foot 3 inch frame never projected either elegance or simplicity. I learned that the ring was a gift from his father, a modest immigrant from Eastern Europe who brought little but his faith from the Urals in 1908. According to family folklore, the ring was a present on my grandfather's eighteenth birthday. I imagine that the ring was acquired at significant sacrifice, as my grandfather turned eighteen at the height of the Great Depression.

I cherish the ring. I look at it often, although I almost never wear it.

I think at some level we all struggle with finding authenticity in our lives—a meaning that transcends the day-to-day stuff and gives us an emotional and historical touchstone. My personal quest probably won't end with my grandfather's signet ring, but there is a gentle certainty in knowing that other than DNA, his ring is probably the only other thing in this world that my great-grandfather, grandfather, father and I have shared—have touched. My son and hopefully his son will eventually share this memento and, through its modest presence, understand that they are part of something that is larger than themselves.

They will never know Harry Aft, nor will his ring ever convey his towering presence, steadfast work ethic or penchant for corny jokes. They will never understand his love of baseball and passion for fresh-squeezed orange juice. What I hope they will understand is that we value his life and understand its relation to our own. Further, I hope they understand that it is not merely the links that make a chain strong, but their interconnectedness that gives them permanence. Harry's signet ring is my link.

David Aft is the father of two sons and the president of the Community Foundation of Northwest Georgia. He has worked in the nonprofit field for over twenty-five years. Aft is a recognized resource and noted speaker on charitable enterprise, civics, fundraising strategy and community development. He is a graduate of the Florida State University School of Social Work where he earned a masters degree in social work in 1987. In his free time, he nurtures his passion for the arts as an active painter and musician.

THE BRICK

WAYNE MINSHEW

The knock on the door was loud and insistent.

"Yeah, what is it?" I said, irritated. I was, after all, involved in a mission of importance: M*A*S*H, and Col. Henry Blake had just been told he was going home.

"I got a package for you," said the voice at the door. He paused, then added, "Sir." It sounded sarcastic.

I opened the door to greet a messenger from UPS.

"Sign here," he said, and I did.

The package was heavy.

"What could it be?" I asked the messenger, who shrugged. "Beats me," he said.

It carried the weight, say, of a bowling ball. But I don't bowl.

"You might open it," said the UPS guy.

I pondered his suggestion, considered it sound and tore into the package, which produced a brick—*a brick?*

Puzzled, I examined the package further and found a note. It was from Claude Felton, who heads-up sports communication at The University of Georgia.

"I was passing by where the field house used to be," he wrote. "They imploded it to make room for a new building, and it's several piles of bricks now. You were the first person I thought of, so I got one for you."

When I was a student-athlete at UGA, I lived in the field house, along with several other baseball players. We lived in the attic. Our furnishings included a bed apiece and a refrigerator. We had somebody in once a week to change the dust.

We were known, if not campus-wide, then certainly within our own confines as Bird, Flap, Hard Man, Hose Nose, Fats, Rocky and Smokey. We lived for baseball, occasionally studied, finally graduated and went separate ways to separate careers.

Now and then, we run into each other and swap memories that we recall as if they happened yesterday instead of five decades ago.

It was the best time of our lives—our glory days.

Since the building housed locker rooms for several sports teams, we had the choice of twenty-five or thirty showers, an abundance of soap and towels, a training room and a smug feeling of privacy set apart from, say, a mundane dormitory.

Also, we—the baseball team—had the only winning team on the UGA campus, adding to our smugness.

The field house was watched over by a watchman we called Hawkshaw, who carried white lightning in a bottle. "It helps me fight off cold winter nights," he told us.

The brick rests on a special table inside my apartment. I had it engraved and added felt tips so it won't damage the table's glass top. It seems cold and impersonal just to look at it, but it contains more memories and causes more reflections than almost anything I own.

I sometimes touch the brick and think back to those heady, glorious times at UGA. They remain the happiest days of my life.

Wayne Minshew is a baseball man through and through. He played baseball for the University of Georgia and in 1958, was team captain. After achieving a journalism degree, he played professional baseball for the St. Louis Cardinals minor league, was a sports writer for the Atlanta Journal Constitution, *and worked as the director of public relations and promotions for the Atlanta Braves. He is the father of a son and daughter, and a grandfather to four grandchildren. In recent years, Wayne's focused his energies on promoting literacy and adult education in Northwest Georgia.*

A TALE OF TWO CLOCKS

MARTHA FORD FRY

From my favorite seat on the couch in my living room, I have a clear view of two clocks. One sits on my mantel and has graced every fireplace in every home I have lived in for nearly thirty years. The other hangs on my kitchen wall. I acquired it just a few years ago. Both represent windows to the relationships I had with the two men connected to them, and, in that sense, this could also be called *A Tale of Two Mikes*.

Mike was what we always called my older brother. When as an adult he would come to be known as the science fiction writer John M. Ford, many would think he had taken a pen name or that the "M" stood for "Michael".

In actuality, the "M" stood for Milo. He was named for his two grandfathers, John Ford and Milo Harley.

A TALE OF TWO CLOCKS

Mike spent many years living in a small, third-floor walk-up in Minneapolis' Wedge District. Mom, Dad, and my younger brother Dale had visited him there a few times. I had not. Mike had become increasingly distant from our family in what would become the last years of his life. I guess when you're in your thirties or forties you feel there will always be an opportunity to make up for lost time. Sadly, in Mike's case, that time never came.

Mike succumbed to a heart attack at the age of forty-nine in 2006. Still in shock, I found myself on a plane meeting my mother and Dale in Minneapolis, making final arrangements for a brother and son none of us had seen in nearly fifteen years.

Entering his apartment, the years of separation disappeared like fog in sunlight.

While there were many aspects of Mike's life that were a mystery to me prior to his untimely death, the brother I knew as a child was reflected in every inch of that one-bedroom apartment.

Reading at the age of two, books were Mike's world long before he wrote his first story. He obtained his first library card at four. On shelves lining every wall in the kitchen, living room, and bedroom, Mike had accumulated his own small library—paperbacks, hard covers, rows of magazines. In some places the shelves jutted out in perpendicular columns just like rows in a library. There were thousands of books, some I recognized from our childhood, some purchased for pennies from library sales, and some gifted and inscribed from famous author-friends. The books were even categorized according to the Dewey Decimal system.

As a child, Mike and Dad shared a penchant for model railroads. At one point, our entire upstairs back porch housed a train layout that remained in a constant state of construction as the two tinkered with their ultimate rail landscape. In Mike's living room HO-scale tracks lined the tops of the bookshelves, circling routes up and back. Boxes of rail cars, landscape props, and building models sat at the ready.

My brother had obviously never lost his aversion to housework or his propensity to be a pack-rat. Every accumulated piece reminded me of the boy who once shared a bunk bed with me.

As I turned and faced the back wall of the living room, my simple recollections of Mike's hobbies and habits melted into deeply held memories of the brother who had perhaps not changed as much as I had once thought.

There, in stark contrast to the clutter and collections filling the rest of the room, a simple wall clock hung prominently and singularly above the littered couch.

In this apartment, which I had never entered during his lifetime, I was immediately reminded of the deep bonds between myself and the brother who had become so inexplicably estranged. Bonds that included the other Milo, the one Mike was named after.

Grandpa Harley, who was also called Mike by all except his children and grandchildren, had been a restaurant man nearly his entire life, working long, but fulfilling, days with my grandmother, his ever-present partner. The restaurant I knew sat on the main drag in North Manchester, Indiana. Unlike most of my cousins who lived near my maternal grandparents, we lived 130 miles away near my dad's folks. Visits to Grandpa and Grandma Harley's also meant visits to Mike's Café. A small town joint, we didn't frequent anything like it at home in the suburbs near Chicago's East Side. Big burly men, most in overalls, sat at the horseshoe counter indulging in five cent cups of coffee while their wives attended quilting bees or Bible studies at the church across the parking lot. It was a family place. Besides my grandparents, my Aunt Hazel and Cousin Peggy would work there. I was occasionally allowed to help at the dishwashing station—a job I relished as a ten year old.

We were treated to pork tenderloin sandwiches and Cocacola. We never drank pop at home, but Mom would let us splurge when we visited our grandparents even though it meant enduring her mother's chastisements regarding our consumption of so much sugary syrup.

Unfortunately, those carefree days were cut short when Grandma Harley succumbed to breast cancer in 1970. She was only fifty-eight; I had just turned eleven. Six months later, Grandpa remarried, and his new wife was not quite as enamored by the restaurant business or with family visits. She soon decided it was time for Grandpa to retire. The restaurant was sold, and they moved to Florida.

Problem was, Grandpa wasn't really ready to retire. Busyness had kept him young, and he enjoyed being productive. It wasn't long before their double-wide had a shingle out front, and Grandpa was repairing clocks.

His interest in intricate time pieces, his pride in craftsmanship, and his love for his family led him to the idea of handcrafting a clock for each of his eight grandchildren—a keepsake for each of us to remember him by. For whatever reason, Grandpa started his endeavor with the girls. As the oldest granddaughter, I became the recipient of the first clock.

A beautiful mantle clock, it is one of the very few personal possessions I cannot imagine myself living without even though it rarely operates any more. The wind-up mechanism lasts less than twenty-four hours, and I lost the struggle to keep it wound on a regular basis years ago.

It may not tell the time, but it represents a significant chapter in the story of my life.

Those visits to Grandma and Grandpa's involved not only the filling of our bellies, but the filling of our souls. They helped shape the parent I would become to my own six children. Trips to Grandma and Grandpa Harley's were lazy days filled with playing *Clue*, building Lincoln Log forts, and jumping from "Grandpa's chair" whenever he entered the family room. It was picking strawberries out of the garden, taffy pulls in the kitchen, Grandpa churning ice cream on the porch, and frightful nights lying on a day bed under a giant deer head, with a five-year old mind ever certain that inevitably that deer would break free from the wall that held him and trample me to death in my sleep.

The love and devotion of the grandpa of my youth ran through the aged fingers of the elderly man I had since made a great grandfather. He embellished my clock with brass knobs and hand-sanded curved edges. A glass door opens to the gold embossed black and white face, harboring guardian angels in the four corners.

My brothers received clocks of a different ilk. By the time Grandpa got around to making clocks for my brothers, his health waned, and I think, too, his spirit.

As a result, Mike and Dale received rough-hewed wooden wall clocks with battery-operated mechanisms and simple, glued-on faces. But I was unaware of this discrepancy until I saw Mike's clock hanging on his wall in his Minneapolis apartment.

The familiar red walnut stain of my clock made Mike's piece instantly recognizable despite the variance in its handiwork. I couldn't help but wonder what memories Grandpa's gift had evoked for Mike.

The oldest grandchild, Mike had taken a vacation with Grandma and Grandpa out west, an opportunity never afforded the rest of us due to Grandma's early death. A scholar from a very young age, Mike enjoyed conversing with the Manchester College boys who boarded at Grandpa's each year. And, books—Grandma and Grandpa's house contained an array of books. While I gravitated towards *The Bobbsey Twins* and *The Boxcar Children*, Mike always seemed to find a more grown-up novel or nonfiction tome to intrigue his ever-inquiring mind.

While my clock may have been more detailed, I found my brother's crudely constructed clock still running. I was struck by the fact that Mike had not only displayed it prominently, he had kept the batteries fresh and, obviously, still used it to report the time of day. Regardless of how strained our personal relationships had become, this clock held evidence that family continued to hold some significance for him.

The clock opened my eyes to see past the disorder of my brother's apartment in other areas, and I was touched by what I found. A Bible our Aunt Marty had given him in elementary school lay on a side table. A newspaper clipping of my own daughters' first published story sat next to his computer. And, in photo boxes, I discovered every letter and birthday card my mother and father had ever written him, some saved for decades and, as indicated from the postal addresses, from numerous residences. Among his treasures was the birth announcement I had sent when my son, the next generation John, was born in 1994.

Once most of the clutter had been cleared, I carefully removed the clock from the wall and gingerly packed it. Back home in Georgia, it immediately took up residence in my kitchen.

The two clocks are mine now; touchstones to both Mikes—the grandfather who gave me an enchanted childhood and the brother who shared those whimsical times. While the latter parts of their lives found them living distantly from the adult

I had become, the two clocks remind me daily that family ties forever bind.

They remain in my heart, as I believe I remained in theirs.

Martha Fry is a freelance writer and editor. A homeschooling mom of six, she writes and speaks on personal finance, single parenting, and spiritual edification. She is a regular contributor to Yahoo!, Wealth Magazine, *and shares insights on her blog,* Dents in My Fender.

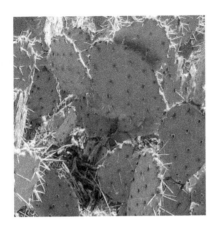

GRANDMA LISSIE'S DEVIL'S EAR

SHERRY POFF

For a few days every summer, my hands bear the marks of working in my cactus. After a morning of pulling weeds, transplanting stray bits, and rearranging the rocks, I find them: tender red pinpricks that I feel when opening toothpaste or turning off a lamp, tiny hair-like bristles that I find when drying off after a shower. I run my hand lightly over my arm to locate the offender then carefully pick it out with tweezers. Sometimes I pull the bristles from my hands with my teeth. It's a risky business, but it's a risk worth running. These miniature needles left in the skin can irritate for days before eventually becoming inflamed. Maybe that's why my family calls this plant, *Devil's Ear*.

In gardening books, the tough, low-growing cactus is listed as eastern prickly pear. In late May—mid-June back in West

Virginia—it bears glossy yellow blossoms, each one opening to the world for one day only, revealing pale red shades at the base of each petal, releasing its brightness into the air before folding into itself forever.

I first became aware of this plant when I found it growing in Grandma's yard. Our Grandma Lissie was a short round woman with graying hair she braided and pinned up in a bun. She bustled about her kitchen and garden, shooing people out of the way and warning against messing things up. Her fussy ways paid off. Everything she cooked and everything she grew was wonderful.

My sister and I always admired Grandma Lissie's plants that grew in the fenced-in yard around her mountaintop farmhouse—an oasis of color surrounded by green fields that seemed to extend to the distant peaks of neighboring mountains. Bright hollyhocks stood against the front fence, yellow and pink snapdragons lined the sidewalk, dahlias of every color were arranged in rows next to pungent spider flowers. Around the side of the house, between beds of yellow and orange marigolds, I discovered the cactus.

Grandma noticed me inspecting her beautiful outdoor plants one day. Just before mom and dad loaded us up to go home, she walked around the house, scissors in hand, clipped off a single leaf pad from the cactus and presented it to me.

"You just bury this in the ground about half-way," she said. "It will make roots and grow."

"Okay. Ow! Thank you." Holding the precious specimen gently between my fingertips, now marked with the first of many small wounds, I wrapped it in the paper provided and carried it to the car for the ride home.

The next day my indulgent parents allowed me to choose any spot I liked for my new plant—my very own cactus. I walked around surveying the possibilities and finally dug a circular bed in the far end of the yard in the grass between our own red and pink dahlias and the spirea along the fence. I scouted along the creek bank to find rocks to form a border around the cactus bed, then—according to Grandma's instructions—buried the prickly leaf half-way. And I waited.

That first summer, the cactus did indeed take root and begin to grow. The next spring it awoke from its winter rest, unwrinkled, and developed even more bright green, prickly pads. By the third summer, I gasped with delight to see flower buds forming, and each June thereafter performed an almost daily count of the yellow blossoms.

I had become a steward of more plants in my family's yard, and although I had taken over much of the watering and work hours each summer pulling weeds from the Jacob's ladder and rock moss, there was a special place in my affection for the barbed beauty in its round bed.

When I went away to college and eventually got married, I left behind my cactus, but came to visit it every summer. Every time I saw it, I felt the old familiar thrill that comes with watching things grow.

My parents moved the plant, somewhat diminished, into a tub, where it persisted in blooming right on time every summer. My sister took a cutting for her home in Kentucky, but I lived in apartments and rental houses—I was still too transient to own and care for outdoor plants.

One fine autumn day, my husband and I at last moved with our four children into a place of our own. Immediately I began surveying my ground to see what I should plant: crocuses and daffodils among the rocks in the corner, dahlias beside the mailbox, zinnias along the fence, and devil's ear cactus in a bed beside the house. My sister brought me a cutting. I put it into the ground and waited.

As did its predecessors, the transplant flourished, and today, it continues to flourish.

In my more southern locale, my cactus blooms early, prompting me to pull the early weeds and rake away the winter's waste so as not to miss a single sunny flower. Even though every encounter with the Devil's Ear is hazardous, I remember why I put up with the sore hands every year as I count the buds and think of the days of pleasure it brings.

One day, as I clipped and rearranged, holding my breath against the stabs I encountered, I realized there was too much for me to keep, so I contacted my daughter, who had moved into a little white house of her own.

"Would you like some of this Devil's Ear cactus?" my text asked.

In less than a minute, I read her reply: "Sure."

"I'll have some ready for you when you come over on Tuesday," I typed.

On Tuesday, Jenny and I met at the park and took a walk. Afterward, she came to my house for lunch. She was about to leave when suddenly she remembered. "Oh, where's that cactus?"

I fetched the pot containing the cuttings.

"Here's what my grandma told me," I said. "Bury this in the ground about halfway, and it will grow."

Jenny smiled, placed the pot carefully in the floor of her car, and drove away.

I stood there and stared into the past seeing my sweet, fussy grandma and myself poking around in her yard. She would love to know that her cactus and her words of wisdom live on and that this plant—so much like her—continues to cheer the lives of us all.

GRANDMA LISSIE'S DEVIL'S EAR

When Sherry Poff isn't puttering around in the flowers, she may be found reading or writing in a sunny spot in the yard. She loves teaching high school English and spending time with her husband, Larry, and their children.

THE BOOK

DOROTHY MCCRORY

When I was an elementary student at Wayne Street School in Lewistown, Pennsylvania in the mid 1940s, I happened upon a treasure trove—not buried treasure, mind you, but nevertheless treasure for which I had to *dig*.

I was in third or fourth grade, and it was the last day of school. Teachers began to clean up their rooms, and as the final bell rang to dismiss us for the summer, I lagged behind and asked my teacher, "What is happening to those books in that box there?"

"Those are discards," she said. "Books that can't be used anymore, so we throw them away."

Incredulous, I asked, "Throw them away!?"

"Oh, yes. Books get worn out and after they've been rebound

once, we have to get ready for new books that will come in over the summer, so we throw the old ones away."

"May I have some of them?" I asked.

"Well, not now. I have to go to a teachers' meeting, but come back in the morning and you can take what you want."

Needless to say, the following day, I was up and dressed and out the door before I could even answer my grandmother's question, "School? On the first day of your vacation?"

When I got there, the doors and windows were open, the janitor was mopping, desks were stacked, teachers were dressed in old clothes. But none of that made an impression on me when I saw the boxes of old books sitting outside each room. Br'er Rabbit to the briar patch. My, my, my! An unbelievable bliss descended over me. If there were buckets of gold, chests filled with jewels, or mountains of dollar bills, nothing could compare to the treasure I saw before me.

"Yes," the teachers said, "Take what you want."

With my arms laden with booty, I made several trips to carry my treasures the three blocks to my house. And wonder of wonders—I found notebooks with unused pages in them and pencils—dozens of pencils. I was set for the summer and then some.

The foray into digging for buried treasure was just the beginning. Every year thereafter, I went back to school the day after the last day, and dug in the boxes to add to my growing library.

All my finds were great, but the most significant book I found happened the day after the last day of my freshman year. I collected a Geometry book and a Latin II book that year with the intention of getting a leg-up on my sophomore year. That good intention went away when I found a book called simply *American Literature*. Published in 1933 (the year I was born) and accessed by Lewistown High School in 1936, *American Literature* began with the *Mayflower Compact* and went into the 20th century.

Poetry, essays, plays, biographies, stories, and documents. I fell in love. I was seduced. There was no way to escape. I met Dickinson, Millay, Teasdale, Poe, Whitman, Whittier, Harte, Alcott, Emerson, Lanier, Lowell (James Russell and Amy), Crane, Sandburg, Kilmer. Not content, however, just to read the poems, I memorized them. *Thanatopsis* by William Cullen Bryant, *The Mountain Whippoorwill* by Stephen Vincent Benet, *Nursery Rhymes for the Tender-Hearted* by Christopher Morley, *I Have a Rendezvous with Death* by Alan Seeger, and on and on. No Latin II or Geometry entered my head that summer. I wallowed in the written word. Shameless, like a wanton hussy, I gave myself to this book called *American Literature*.

That was 1947, over fifty years ago, and where is that book? Right beside me as I write this story. When I left Lewistown in 1951 to move to New York City to attend college, the book went with me. When I moved to New Jersey to teach, so too moved the book. When I joined the army and was stationed at Ft. McClellan, Alabama, the book was stationed there, too. And when I settled in Dalton, Georgia in 1963, the book settled, too.

In many ways, the book shaped my life. I know I can trace my love of literature to what I discovered between its frayed and tattered covers. When I am cremated at my life's end, I ask that some kind soul slip the book along with me to the crematorium, then the book and I, so long inseparable, will be inseparable forever.

Dot McCrory is a retired high school counselor and English teacher. Coming from a family of poets and storytellers, she carries on the tradition by writing a poem each month for her women's literary club. "Actually," she says, "It's standup comedy in poetic form."

BLUE PLATE SPECIAL

JANE STARNER

We sat on metal folding chairs holding our numbered paddles waiting to bid on memories of Aunt Marty's life. The auctioneer stood on a raised platform in the armory, his sleeves rolled up, babbling in the hypnotic way auctioneers learn before the climatic "Going once, going twice, sold!"

My cousins, my son and I bravely raised our paddles to bid on antique furniture and dishes. Sometimes we were rewarded with copper luster pitchers, blue flow plates, a fourposter bed, and a mirrored hall tree. Frequently we were outbid.

Hours passed. The auctioneer's voice grew hoarse. He wiped his forehead more frequently. The Church of the Brethren ladies began putting away food and cleaning the kitchen. Patiently, I waited for a table containing miscellaneous treasures:

mismatched costume jewelry, Ball canning jars, an old wooden decoy, a decorative schooner and a simple blue plate bearing the raised head of a woman. I wanted the plate in spite of the two small chips. No one else bid higher than my one dollar. *It was mine.*

"Why did you buy that plate?" asked my daughter-in law. I explained that my mother had had a plate exactly like it; somehow it was lost. Cousin Connie joined the conversation: "My dad had a plate like that, too. Originally there were six. Grandmother gave him and each sibling a plate."

In our home, birthdays were never a huge event. No clowns. No pony rides. No parties with crepe paper streamers and balloons. No matching paper tablecloths and napkins. No upright piano—not even an out-of-tune one with yellowed keys. Instead, on our birthdays, the blue plate appeared, holding a homemade, perhaps lopsided, cake with icing and candles, a rarity during the war years when sugar was rationed. I licked the icing from the face of the blue woman before washing the plate in the sink and replacing it in the hutch cupboard.

We never questioned the identity of the stern woman on the plate, but she stared out at us, surrounded by three circles embossed on the blue. Her name "Frances E. Willard" was barely legible below the dates "1839-1939." I wondered about this unsmiling woman with hair pulled into a bun. Connie said that Willard was once president of the Woman's Christian Temperance Union (WCTU) and was active in the woman's suffrage movement. She was also president of a women's college in Chicago and the first dean of women when Northwestern University admitted women.

Grandmother received the set of plates in gratitude for her work in the Indiana chapter of the WCTU and in the suffrage movement. At that time, activists believed if women were allowed to vote, prohibition could become law.

Perplexed, I mused on how little we know of others—even relatives. Grandmother was a plain woman who wore dark clothes, cotton hose, sensible shoes, and no makeup. For church, she added a lace collar and a simple brooch. When cooking, she pinned a calico apron to her bosom. I remember her gigantic fern kept on a stand near the southern windows lined with velvety African violets in shades of pink and purple.

When I stayed at Grandma's, we played Chinese checkers or sat on the porch swing counting cars. I never saw her without her prayer veil or sun bonnet, except at night when she removed the tortoise-shell combs and hair pins from her bun and brushed her long grey strands, saving hair from the brush in a flowered porcelain jar with a hole in the top. That saved hair would be used as stuffing for pin cushions. In truth, Grandma Snider looked a bit like the woman on the blue plate.

I could not imagine this soft-spoken matron marching, carrying signs, or picketing for women's votes. Certainly, she was no Carrie Nation, carrying an ax into bars. Perhaps she had, like Maud Gonne, a pilgrim spirit. This may have attracted my handsome grandfather. A young teacher and minister, G. A. Snider was known for his impressive appearance and his forceful speaking. He stood up for his pacifist views and became a strict but loving parent, forbidding drinking, smoking, dancing, card playing and movie going. Still, my mother and her siblings became a fun-loving, rowdy bunch.

People were leaving the armory, loading dishes into boxes and tying furniture on pick-up trucks and in vans. As we said our goodbyes, I held tight to the chipped plate, knowing it would continue to hold our birthday cakes and our memories. I promised myself I would pass on to my children and grandchildren the deeds of my Grandmother Snider and of Francis Willard, the face in the special blue plate.

JANE STARNER

Jane Starner is a retired teacher of English and drama who travels the world looking for her next great adventure. She's been a docent at the Hunter Museum and a carver of carousel animals at Horsin' Around in Chattanooga, Tennessee. Jane has finished a memoir for her grandchildren chronicling her life up to age twenty-one when she began teaching. She writes poetry and children's stories.

CARNIVAL GLASS

NANCY RATCLIFFE

"Finally, I have a place to put these!" I told my husband as I put the finishing touches on our new home's guest bathroom by placing a pair of Carnival glass pieces on the vanity. The iridescent glassware once belonged to my paternal grandmother, Emma Ralston Duvall.

Sam and I were enjoying decorating our new home. It was the house where we planned to grow old—our *forever* house.

"All this time, I've never had a place where these really fit, but they look great in here," I added, quite pleased with their placement.

The shiny *treasures* didn't really seem like treasures to me more than thirty years ago when I was presented with them. Shortly after my wedding, my mother and father visited my oldest first cousin, and before the end of their time together, she handed them a shoebox tied together with twine.

"This is Nancy's wedding present," Cousin Bonnie said. "I've had these since Grandma died because I was the oldest, and now that Nancy's married, it's her turn to have them. After all, she's named after Grandma: Nancy Emma."

A few days later, my mother gave me the box. I was anxious to discover the contents—*until I saw them.*

"What is this?" I asked examining the two pieces of dark purple glassware. I had no idea the purpose of either piece, and nothing in our apartment matched the rather strange colors.

"I remember when Grandma bought those," my father said. "We were living at Curryville in Gordon County, and she got those from the rolling store."

Though I wasn't old enough to have ever shopped from the rolling store, I had always been fascinated by the idea of a traveling merchant and his wares since we visited an elderly relative in Kentucky's coal-mining country whose store was still parked in his yard long after he had given up his route. Most of what was left in the dilapidated truck was a combination of castoffs from their home and some Watkins products like linament and vanilla flavoring. That image, along with the times I had seen the *Goatman* and his wagonload of treasures bring traffic to a standstill on Georgia's Highway 41, made me more interested in my father's recollection.

"I think she must have bought those about 1914, when I was about five years old," my dad recalled. "She saved and saved to buy those. I think she must have paid five or ten cents for each piece, which was a small fortune back then."

He pointed to one of the objects.

"This little thing that looks like a vase is a hatpin holder," he explained.

I picked-up the other piece. It looked like a candy dish with a lid.

"And that's a jelly jar," he continued. "Before refrigeration, jellies stayed on the table between meals."

I nodded with understanding. Even in my childhood, Aunt Mell, one of the last of the great farm wives, had simply spread a tablecloth over the leftovers that wouldn't spoil. Anytime I visited, I peered under the cloth and filched one of her cold homemade biscuits for a snack.

"It was awfully nice of Bonnie to give me these," I told my parents. What I *didn't* say was that at that point in my life, I would have preferred a piece of china or crystal to some antiques that didn't match anything in my new décor. I dutifully wrote the thank you note and placed the box in the top of the closet and forgot about it.

We moved twice before we settled into our first brand new home. Each time the box went with us and was placed high on a shelf, out of sight, out of mind. Once again, the deep greenish purple colors and the very ornate Victorian design seemed out of place in the gray and mauve color scheme of the mid 1980s.

But by that time, I had lost both my mother and father, sold the family home, and unearthed the remains of my grandparent's meager possessions. As sharecroppers who never owned land of their own, my grandparents had left nothing of great value. I had only bits and snatches of memories of the woman for whom I had been named, and I had never known my grandfather, who died before my birth. As a tribute to my family, I found a spot on an obscure shelf in the living room and placed my keepsakes there.

Gradually, I began to understand how treasured those pieces of Carnival glass were and to appreciate my grandmother's love of beauty. In her old trunk, damaged by the ravages of weather,

I found beautiful needlework, though I was only able to salvage scraps of her crocheted doilies and tatting. Emma was a woman who never owned a home of her own and who died without enough money for a tombstone. The rare relics of beauty I found made me appreciate the struggles she had endured throughout her life—two World Wars, the Depression, and being the only female in a house with seven men.

After placing the glassware on the vanity of our new home's bathroom where the colors were compatible, I hardly thought about them and never questioned whether they were of any value. I was simply happy to have a place to display them.

When a friend came to see my new home, she spotted the pieces.

"Where did you get those?" she asked. "They're very valuable, you know. If you ever decide to sell them, please let me know."

She continued to emphasize their value until finally I asked, "Exactly what are they worth?"

She promised to look up the value and get back to me. A few days later, she called to say that the two pieces were valued at $800.

No one is still living who recalls any of the specifics of my grandmother's glassware purchase, and there is no one to share the unexpected good news of the pair's value. In a time when most of our purchases are disposable and outdated before we get home from the store with them, I find it ironic that it took more than eighty years for someone to appreciate Emma's treasures, and for them to become the most valuable possessions she ever owned.

Now when I pass by the counter where the pieces sit, I often smile and think that in my next home, I'll have to decorate a room *around* the Carnival glass. I am reminded of the many treasures passed down to me, and I become a bit sentimental and regret that it took me so long to appreciate my grandmother's longing to own something elegant. My suspicion is that my love for china and all things beautiful was passed down to me from Grandmother Emma. She would marvel that today's rolling store comes to me via FedEx, UPS or the US Postal Service, each delivering packages I've ordered online or from a TV shopping show. If Grandma were still here, she'd probably love QVC and the treasures she'd find there.

Nancy Ratcliffe spent much of her childhood listening to the stories and conversations of her older relatives, absorbing all of the Southern wit and wisdom they espoused. A retired educator, Nancy says that one of the most important items on her "bucket list" is writing and sharing the stories of her family. "The greatest compliment my students ever gave me was that I made writing easy," Nancy says. "I always told them: It is easy—once you get started. So recording my memories is simply practicing what I preached for all those years."

THE PICTURE HAT

JANIE DEMPSEY WATTS

Mama and I were at the final fitting for my wedding gown. The seamstress, Madame, a bouncy French woman, held up a skein of pink ribbon next to my face.

"Pink is much better for your skin tone, don't you think, Mademoiselle?" asked Madame in her heavily-accented English.

"Yes," I answered.

But I really wasn't thinking about the trim for my wedding gown. Instead, I kept wondering who would "give me away" during the wedding ceremony. Originally I had asked my father and he had agreed but later changed his mind. Although my parents had been divorced for several years, emotions still ran high.

Mama's thick southern drawl interrupted my thoughts. "Can we see the hat?" Mama asked.

THE PICTURE HAT

Reared as a southern belle, Mama had thrown herself full throttle into my wedding plans. She envisioned a "Gone With the Wind" style ensemble. Madame brought over a round hatbox and placed it on Mama's lap with a dramatic flourish.

"Voila," she said, gesturing for Mama to open the lid. Mama gently removed the lid and pulled out the widest brimmed hat I'd ever seen. I reached in and pulled out the hat, placed it on my head and turned so Mama could see. She clapped her hands together and sighed.

"Perfect," she said.

But I wasn't so sure. With its layers of lace and ribbon, the hat seemed a bit frilly. And that brim—broad enough to use as an umbrella. Excited about my over-sized chapeau, Mama chatted with the seamstress as she pinned on pink ribbon. Mama hadn't had a fancy wedding herself and she seemed so excited about my southern belle ensemble. I glanced into the mirror at the picture hat and the wide hem of my gown—so old-fashioned, but not that bad. Besides, it was too late to order anything else. I turned my thoughts to my other dilemma—would I end up giving myself away?

A week before the wedding Mama and I had dinner with my future in-laws. Learning of my dilemma, my father-in-law-to-be graciously offered to be my escort.

"I'd be proud to walk you down the aisle," he stated in his husky voice, gazing at me with his deep brown eyes.

I appreciated his offer, and his sincerity made me want to cry, but I couldn't let him. How could he "give the bride away" when he wasn't my family, not yet? We discussed an uncle but none felt right for the task. No solution seemed in sight until my fiancé, Steve, spoke.

"Why does it have to be a man?" he asked.

I thought about it. It was the late seventies, but most of the weddings I'd ever attended had been steeped in tradition. I'd never seen anyone except a man perform the hand-off. My future father-in-law shook his head in dismay, clearly disapproving of his son's idea. Steve reached out and touched Mama's shoulder.

"I think you should do it," said Steve. Mama beamed, but I didn't know what to say.

"I'd love to," Mama said, "if the bride wants me to." Everyone turned to look at me and I looked back at Mama. A petite five foot two inches, she seemed to have grown an inch taller at the mere suggestion.

"Why not?" I said. Mama grinned. I smiled too, but thought it wasn't a good idea. I'd never seen a mother give away the bride.

A week later at the rehearsal, Mama went through the paces flawlessly. But still, I worried about our wedding day. What would our guests think?

The wedding day arrived. A bit nervous, I processed down the aisle of the church. Wrapped in a cloud of rainbow pastel voile, Mama calmly waited for me in the front. Seeing her, I moved ahead confidently. She stepped out of the pew and into the aisle to offer me her arm. Together, we walked over to my groom. Then she did something she hadn't rehearsed. She took both his hands in hers, looked him hard in the eyes as if to say, "You had better take good care of my daughter."

After the wedding, when we were taking pictures, Mama leaned in under the hat's wide brim to give me a kiss. When she pulled away, the hat tipped and almost fell off, but Mama helped me put it back on. We both laughed at the "tipsy hat."

In the reception line, everyone congratulated Mama on doing a good job giving me away. My picture hat was a big hit.

Today, when I look at the frilly hat, I can see Mama's proud smile and hear her laughter. With its lace and ribbon, the picture hat is delicate and traditional, so unlike Mama, a woman ahead of her time, brave enough to carry off a "man's job" with such dignity and grace.

Janie Watts is still happily married to the fellow her mama gave her away to. Her first novel, Moon Over Taylor's Ridge *(Little Creek Books) came out in fall of 2012. Her stories have appeared in five Chicken Soup for the Soul books,* The Ultimate Gardener, Guideposts, Stories to Warm a Grandma's Heart, Georgia Backroads, *and in* Catoosa Life Magazine, *where she has her own column. Her short stories (fiction) have appeared in* Southern Women's Review, Blue Crow Magazine, *and* A Tapestry of Voices. *She may be reached at www.JanieWatts.com.*

JONATHAN'S BIBLE AND MARGARET'S WAX VINE

JIM GILREATH

I did not know my great-grandfather or great-grandmother but always felt that I did from my grandmother's stories about them. Both Jonathan Jeremiah Gilreath and Margaret Hutson were children of the mountains, born and reared in the 1800s in a highland valley near the small community of Suches in Union County, Georgia. It was there in that remote place, nearer to the sky than to any city or town, that they met, married and went about the business of farming, keeping house, having children, and preaching the word of God.

My great-grandfather's grandfather's grandfather had arrived in the British colonies of North America around 1700 from Aberdeenshire, Scotland. Through the years, wars were fought, governments overthrown and new ones created, and the red man cruelly removed from an ancestral home in the mountains, but not before leaving a legacy of native American blood in my family's DNA, both from my great-grandmother, and from my great-great-grandmother. The men in my family at that time appeared so strikingly Native American, that they would not have been out of place as extras in an old western film.

My great-grandfather was a circuit-riding Baptist preacher, who took time out from being a farmer, a husband, and a father to bring salvation to the ungodly in the north Georgia hills in buggy and on horseback. His own father died in the Civil War, near the Cumberland Gap, on the South's retreat from the Battle of Perryville, Kentucky, leaving a widow and nine children, my great-grandfather being one of the younger.

It was before this in the 1840s that my great-grandfather's grandfather reigned as king of the bootleggers in Union County, finding it easier and more profitable to convert corn to corn liquor, than hauling it over the mountains to mill and market in Dahlonega. I do not know whether these or other circumstances were the reasons for my great-grandfather being called to serve his Lord and Savior, but he served faithfully until his death in 1930, his old King James Bible always by his side. At the time of his death, he was the longest-serving Baptist minister in the North Georgia Baptist Association.

This is a story of keepsakes—not one, but two—one from each of my great-grandparents. From my great-grandfather comes a religious keepsake, his Bible. It was the only book he owned, yet all he needed. He could read very little, if any, so by fire and lamplight he had his oldest daughters read to him every evening after supper. The old words of the worn King James edition rang off the cabin walls, while outside, the cold, night winds howled down off the mountain. Sometimes on those cold nights, he would come home from his church on horseback, and call out to his children to bring the hammer to break his boots free from ice that had accumulated on the stirrups from the creeks he had crossed, before he could dismount.

From my great-grandmother comes an ancient yet amazingly, a still living thing. This keepsake is a plant that is technically at least 130 years old, perhaps older. The wax vine (a cultivar of the genus Hoya) is a houseplant that originally grew in a large pot sitting on the edge of her porch so that it might be easily moved under shelter during cold, mountain winters. Its journey, as well as the my great-grandfather's old Bible, had many twists and turns, but ultimately, both found their way to me.

The old Bible and the wax vine left Suches in 1905 with the family, by covered wagon pulled by two steers, up over the mountain and down into Dahlonega. The journey to Walton County took nearly two weeks with the family stopping and camping under the stars each evening. Most landowners along the route were hospitable and allowed camping and watering of livestock, but some did not. Once or twice, my great-grandfather provided a secret handshake of the Masonic brotherhood, making reluctant landowners only happy to open their homes to the wayfarers. After a hundred miles or so, and many adventures, the Bible and the wax vine came to the community of Gratis in Walton County.

Once there, my great-grandparents got on with the business of farming and preaching, much as in the mountains, only in a more hospitable environment. The soil was better, the winters milder, and the children old enough now to contribute. There were also people in the Gratis community who needed to hear the word of God and to be saved, married, and buried. The old Bible was still read aloud in the evenings by a younger daughter and the wax vine grew happily at the edge of the porch.

JONATHAN'S BIBLE AND MARGARET'S WAX VINE

Many years later, my great-grandparents, and their only remaining child still at home, left Walton County and made another journey to the small community of Smarr in Monroe County, Georgia. Both in their seventies, they still farmed, kept house and preached. When health issues arose, my grandfather, grandmother, and my dad's older sister, (my dad not yet born), moved to Smarr to live with and care for them.

My great-grandmother died of cancer in 1923. My great-grandfather then walked away from the farm and returned to live in the old mountain cabin home place until 1930 when he became ill and died. After his death, the Bible and the wax vine went home with my grandparents to Bay Creek community in Walton County, the Bible placed in a drawer and only taken out to record life events on those hallowed, center pages. The wax vine grew safely in a pot on the porch.

As a child visiting my grandparent's house, I liked to search through dresser drawers out of curiosity.

"That young'un is rambling again," my mother was fond of saying.

The old leather Bible was familiar to me in its place inside the drawer in the hallway of my grandparent's old house. I loved the smell of it, the smooth, worn feel of its leather cover, the pages inside written by goose quill pen that listed births, deaths, and marriages, and the fire and brimstone hellfire that came from the Book of Revelations, that I dared not read too much of, less a rider on a pale horse come up to my window as I slept. Years later, after the deaths of my grandparents, the Bible came to my dad, and after he and my mom's death, it came to me. But the wax vine traveled a different road.

Folks in times past gave each other cuttings or rootings of favorite plants. These are known collectively as *pass-along plants*. At some point in time, my grandmother gave a rooting of the wax vine to her younger sister who lived nearby. The plant flourished at my great aunt's house on her porch where it remained until her death, then was passed to her daughter, my first cousin once removed. Years later in 2011, my mom passed away and my cousin came to the visitation. On that evening, she told me that there was something in her car that belonged to me. I went to her car, opened the door, and saw a plant in a pot, carefully wrapped in plastic on the floorboard. It was a beautiful wax vine. She said that it had been my great-grandmother's plant.

Life is filled with cycles and circles and two of my dearest keepsakes have found their way home to me from great-grandparents I never knew. These keepsakes came from a time and place far removed from my iPad, my iPhone, and the Internet.

Yet in some ways, the stories and places associated with these keepsakes are more real to me than anything in my life today. As I sit here tonight, holding this old Bible, in my house, not five miles or so from where Jonathan and Margaret Hutson Gilreath lie side-by-side in New Providence Church cemetery, a church where he preached in the 1920s, I think about those cold nights long ago in the mountains and my great-grandfather and grandmother there by the fireplace. It is as if the years just melt away and I can close my eyes and almost remember.

Jim Gilreath is a retired high school science teacher who now spends much of his time in a porch swing watching the days go by. He has a continued interest in all aspects of the natural world, especially birds and bird photography. He is past president and current member of the Ocmulgee Audubon Society in Macon, Georgia, a member of the Georgia Ornithological Society, and newsletter editor of the Central Georgia Vintage Chevrolet Club of America. He is the current sponsor and organizer of the annual "Descendants of William Gilreath Reunion" held near Dawsonville, Georgia. He lives with his wife, Sandy, a retired math teacher and award-winning quiltmaker, and their Welsh Corgi, Tasha, in a house, back-in-the-woods, near Bolingbroke, Georgia.

UNDEFEATED: THE CAST

PEGGY GILBERT

A yellowed wrist cast sits like a proud trophy on a bookshelf in our basement family room. You might ask who in their right mind would save a cast? We all know how sweaty and stinky casts get over time. And besides, why would anyone want to remember all the drama and trauma associated with a broken bone? But this particular cast has a story to tell.

Our son, Tom broke his wrist going up for an easy lay-up eighteen years ago. As he drove to the basket, a Whitko player fouled him hard, and he came crashing down into the stands at the end of the court under the goal. In the split second it took for his left hand to bounce off the floor and take the brutal impact of his entire body, all his basketball dreams came to a screeching halt.

And so this cast is not just any old cast. No—this cast is a memory. It's a work of art. It was sculpted to fit our son's eighteen-year-old hand with a wide opening for his four left fingers and a neat hole for his left thumb. There is a slit down the center taped neatly to make it removable so he could wear it for protection after the bones had mended. This cast made it possible for Tom to get back on the court and play basketball again.

Our son's love for basketball started even before he went to kindergarten. We raised our family in the small town of North Manchester, just a bit south and due west of Ft. Wayne, Indiana. That's right, Indiana—the state best known for its Hoosier Hysteria during every basketball season. To this day, my husband's comment regarding new born babies is always the same, whether it's a boy or a girl: "Very cute! But does the baby have a jump shot?"

Life revolved around that bright orange ball and the hoop mounted from our carport. If you ever drive through Indiana, just count the basketball goals whether free standing in parking lots or playgrounds, or mounted on garages, barns and sheds. You will soon lose count.

In grade school, recess was basketball time. At home, when there was no one around to play with, Tom shot free throws by the hundreds. And there were summer leagues and basketball camps and open gyms.

Just try to imagine how ecstatic he was when he got to play with the Manchester Squires Junior Varsity team as a freshman. Known for his three-point shot and ranked second in the state for free throw shooting, he was a respected player, but he certainly wasn't alone in his ardor for basketball. Four other players shared his skill and passion, and that particular Squire team came together in a winning combination that North Manchester had not seen for many years, and for that matter, has not seen since. They just *clicked*.

In fact they worked together so beautifully, that in his junior year, they made it all the way to the semi-state finals, also known lovingly as the Sweet Sixteen, which signifies the final sixteen teams left in the Indiana state high school basketball tournament. And this was when Indiana still played in a single-class tournament. Though they were ranked third in the state that year, they were defeated in the first game of the semi-state tournament by South Bend Clay, a big city team that ended up winning the whole kit and caboodle. As a matter of fact, three of Clay's players ended up in the NBA.

And so Tom and his teammates began their senior year and final season with high hopes. By January, they were still undefeated in the season and everybody in town was just electrified with excitement and anticipation at the beginning of every game—especially games on our home court. His team lost only three games in two years and they *never* lost a game on their home court.

Our biggest local rival, the Whitko Wildcats, was playing on our home court right after the Christmas holiday and the gym was standing room only. Our Squires were comfortably ahead with just seconds left in the fourth quarter when Tom got the pass and went in for that lay-up. Somebody undercut him, and he went crashing down. As noisy as the crowd was, there are people who told me later that they actually heard his bone snap.

All I remember was seeing my husband leap from his seat and run around the court toward the home team's bench.

"Oh yeah, it's broken all right," a guy behind me said, giving me an urgent shove.

"You should get over there, too," he prodded.

Angry with the *messenger*, I countered, "It is NOT broken!" and in a sort of daze, I followed my husband.

UNDEFEATED: THE CAST

When I got to Tom, the trainer had already placed an inflatable cast on his arm, and they were pumping it up. My son was in hideous pain. The final buzzer signaled the end of the game and another victory, but it was weird how quiet the gym seemed as I stepped back helplessly to get out of the way. Tom draped his six foot three inch sweaty frame over the short little female manager as she tried to keep his injured arm erect and walk with him back to the locker room.

I could expand on the trip to the hospital, the recovery, the therapy, the well-wishers, the cards, but it's the remainder of the season that justifies why his cast is on the shelf. This kid—our son—went back to practice the following Monday. He couldn't shoot. He couldn't pass, and he sure as heck couldn't catch a pass. So what did he do? He did the only thing he *could* do. He ran. He ran in the gym. He ran up and down the tiered stadium seats. He ran through the halls of the school. He just ran and ran and ran. There were eight games left in the season, and so he spent his practice time running.

He couldn't even dress out. He sat on the bench in his sport jacket and khakis and helped with stats while his dad and I swallowed hard every time the team charged on to the floor to play yet another game as Tom walked in with the trainers and coaching staff.

By the last game, the healing was well underway, but it was excruciating to catch a pass. The doctor sculpted a cast for him just for that purpose, and I'll never forget the standing ovation he got when he swished his first three-pointer after what seemed like an endlessly long basketball hiatus. Our Squires ended their senior year undefeated and eager to begin sectional play.

It was then that it occurred to me that Tom had taught us a life lesson—a lesson about perseverance, courage and poise. Today this thirty-six-year-old guy chuckles at the reminder of that experience. During a visit home for Christmas with his wife and four-year-old daughter, he noticed the cast and said, "Wow Mom, I can't believe you kept that old thing all these years!"

But when I fold laundry, work on a sewing project, or do a little ironing, I smile when I look up at the yellowed wrist cast. I remember getting some laughs when I filled it with red carnations and used it as a centerpiece for his graduation open house. Stuffed inside is a piece of paper listing everyone who sent cards, called or visited during that time. Of course, I will keep this humble keepsake forever. Perhaps I will even have it bronzed one day. After all, it gives the word "undefeated" a whole new meaning.

Retired English teacher Peggy Gilbert lives in a small town in northern Indiana where she and her husband, Bob, raised two children—Tom and Sarah. She enjoys reading, sewing, mowing, planting, weeding and dragging the garden hose around. But even more, she loves to hang out with her grand daughters, four-year-old Carley in Maryland and two-year-old Lily in Missouri.

NANNY'S MAGIC PAN

MITZI BOYD

As a child, I knew that I could count on my Nanny Keith for numerous things that I might need. These things included Kleenex tissue in her dress pocket for a runny nose or tears, half a stick of Juicy Fruit gum, and a simple butter pound cake that was out of this world.

I was the recipient of her delicious chocolate-frosted pound cake every year for my birthday. From the age of five, when my family returned to Tennessee to live until I enlisted in the United States Navy at twenty, Nanny always provided the foundation for the birthday celebration. They weren't fancy cakes like you buy in the store. They were decorated very simply with hard candy pieces that spelled out "Happy Birthday," and even though it didn't cost a lot to make, to me it couldn't have been more special. It was a certainty that at sometime during a visit home I would have my "birthday" cake no matter what the month. It was always the highlight of my trip.

It was a blessing to have my grandmother living when my son was born, so he, too, had the privilege of tasting her delicious treat. Even after I learned that it was not a special recipe of any sort, still I knew there was something about it that was different. I have had pound cake in many places, yet none tasted quite as good.

After Nanny's death, my mother and her siblings began the unavoidable task of dividing her things. I asked for only a few items that I had given to her through the years, and I asked for *the* cake pan.

It was surrendered without any argument, and frankly, I was surprised that the many years of wonderful cakes did not seem to mean as much to my cousins and siblings as they did to me. Nevertheless, I was thrilled with my treasure. Its shiny dented surface with scratch marks from all those years comforts me. It transports me to a place in my heart filled with love and joy—it takes me back to my childhood.

I was convinced that the secret of Nanny's extraordinary cakes had to be in *the pan*. That was the only plausible explanation. The mix came from a box—nothing added to it or taken away—purchased from the local supermarket, so I knew the magic wasn't in the ingredients. I had watched her make her cakes so many times over the years, and I knew how it was done. Of course, I watched her make dumplings and gravy too, but still can't make either very well.

And so, it was with some trepidation that I mixed up my first pound cake to bake in Nanny's pan. What if I was wrong, and the magic wasn't in the pan? Would I ever be able to replicate that wonderful sweet, buttery taste that floods my mind with memories if she didn't leave the magic there?

I followed the directions just as I had watched her do, greasing the pan and dusting it with flour so it wouldn't stick. My mind traveled back to all the times I watched her hands perform the very same tasks. She cracked the eggs a certain way and filled the pan with a pool of batter. Then, when the cake was frosted, she always allowed my brothers and me to lick the icing from the bowl.

I placed the pan in the oven. It was a long time, or so it seemed, until the cake was done. I took it out of the oven and let it cool just enough to get it out of the pan. I was impatient to taste it, and I decided to taste it while it was still warm—it's better that way. As soon as I took the first bite, I was reminded of Nanny in her kitchen. I revisited my past for a moment. The cake tasted exactly as it did when she made it for us as children—even my brothers and my mother agreed.

I have made pound cake many times over the years since Nanny passed away, yet every time I take the pan out of the cabinet, I see her as plainly as if I was a child again. Her short, stout body with her hands gnarled from arthritis and her colorful house dresses that were the staple of her wardrobe. The image causes me sadness and joy at the same time.

Today, I bake birthday cakes for my own grandchildren in that same dented metal pan—I think Nanny would be happy about that. I know it is the love from all the cakes she baked for me in the pan that continues to give each new pound cake that same special sweetness.

Nanny left the magic for me in the pan after all—another thing I just knew I could count on her for.

Mitzi Boyd is a mother, grandmother, daughter, sister, friend, writer, athlete and baker of Nanny's Magic Pound Cakes. She has worked in the nonprofit and healthcare industry for nearly thirty years, specializing in financial management and office administration. She is a proud veteran of the United States Navy and lives in Northwest Georgia with a small band of animal companions.

LUCKY LOTTERY NUMBERS

AUDREY LANIER ANDERSEN

I pulled my navy blue Ford Explorer into the garage and quickly shut the overhead door to seal out the sweltering heat. It was August in Southern Illinois. The heat and humidity rivaled anything I had ever experienced in my seventeen years growing up in Middle Georgia.

I had just escorted my parents to the airport in St. Louis and driven the twenty-five miles back to my home in O'Fallon, Illinois. I stepped inside my kitchen, draped my purse over the back of a chair, and reached across the counter to hang my keys on the hook—that's when I noticed the single scrap of pale blue paper. I studied it. It had been torn hastily from my notepad, and left deliberately on the center of my desk with a twenty dollar bill. Written on the piece of paper were two rows of numbers:

AUDREY LANIER ANDERSEN

2—6—9—19—30—33 ($10)
8—13—28—36—43—47 ($10)

I recognized my father's rushed handwriting and instantly understood what he had secretly left there for me to find upon my return.

I glanced at the clock and preformed some quick calculations in my head. My parents had surely touched down safely at the Atlanta airport by now and been greeted at their gate by my sister. Amber was responsible for helping them navigate the airport labyrinth and for driving them back to their home in Warner Robins, Georgia.

Standing alone in my kitchen, I smiled at the idea of playing Daddy's lottery numbers for him. It was 1992 and at that time Georgia did not have a state lottery, but Illinois did. The possibility, albeit remote, of winning a $10 million jackpot intrigued my father. He had always been a bit of a gambling man—hustling unsuspecting men at local pool and billiard halls and taking his friends' petty cash in late night games of poker. Playing the lottery was right up his alley, and the numbers written on that scrap of paper represented the extravagant dreams of a fifty-eight-year-old man.

I examined the digits closely. While the second row of numbers appeared to be completely random, the first row of numbers was familiar to me—each of those numbers represented a birth date of a member of our family. A sudden revelation ensued: my dad's lucky numbers were our birthdays.

My older brother, Andy, was born on December 2. My younger sister, Amber, was born on August 6. The numbers 9, 19 and 30 are the respective birth dates of my mother, my father and me. The last number on that line, 33, represents the year in which my father was born.

My parents were traditional, middle class people who had been born and raised during the Great Depression in rural south Georgia. Both Mom and Dad were brought up in families of meager financial means, but both were raised in large, loving families rich in southern values, work ethics, and pride.

My parents said their vows in early December of 1956, and together, they raised three children. Like our parents, my brother, sister and I did not have a lavish upbringing, but we did enjoy the devotion of two loving parents who worked hard and made sacrifices so we could live comfortably. My dad worked two jobs to support our family and my mom worked from home as a bookkeeper. This allowed her to keep us properly supervised, well fed and safely chauffeured to our many extracurricular commitments.

We lived in a subdivision in a modest three bedroom, two bathroom house where we spent our summers riding bikes with neighborhood friends, picking wild plums and blackberries along a dirt road behind our house, and playing summer sports at a park just down the street. Although we never took elaborate vacations during those summer months, I never felt like I was missing out on anything. From time to time, my dad would contemplate driving across country to visit the Grand Canyon or the California coast. His fondest desire was to one day travel to the icy, foreign landscape of Alaska, but the reality of raising three kids, working two jobs and eventually paying for all three of us to attend Georgia Tech prevented them from traveling to far away places.

The summer of 1992 would be different. My dad had recently retired from Robins Air Force Base where he worked for thirty-four years as a supervisor on the flight line in the Air Freight Terminal. All three of us kids had, by 1992, graduated from college and flown out of our parents' nest. For the first time in their lives my parents were now free to pursue some of their dreams that had been long postponed. I had been living in the Midwest for the preceding three years and had not made as many trips home to visit my family as I should have. That particular summer, airfares from Atlanta to St. Louis were unusually low, making it cheaper and quicker to fly than to drive. So, with the encouragement of my sister, my parents boarded an airplane bound for St. Louis to visit my husband and me.

During their five day stay with us, we did the things that most tourists visiting the area would do: we saw the famous St. Louis Arch and marveled at the size and strength of the Mighty Mississippi—both sights my parents had seen only in photographs. I took them on a driving tour of Scott Air Force Base where I worked as a negotiator for the Department of Defense. My mother is an avid gardener, and on their last full day there, we toured the Botanical Gardens in St. Louis. My dad was not feeling well that day, and instead of braving the near 100 degree temperatures that afternoon, he stayed at our home and watched a baseball game on television in air conditioned comfort.

On their last night with us, we enjoyed a quiet dinner-and-a-movie night at home. The first movie we watched was *My Girl*, and I remember being somewhat uneasy about its somber storyline. Thankfully, the second film we viewed was a comedy, and it quickly lightened our moods. My dad laughed so hard that tears ran down his cheeks as he watched Macaulay Culkin's character abuse the two would-be thieves in the movie *Home Alone*. It was a very happy ending to their visit with us.

The next morning, Mom and Dad hastily packed, shoved their bags into my car, and we left so that they could catch an early flight. I walked them to their gate and waited until they were called to board. I hugged them both goodbye and watched as my parents disappeared down the jetway. And then I boarded my own vehicle, and made the forty-five minute drive back to O'Fallon pleased that I was able to enjoy some quality time with my parents and content in knowing I would see them again in three short months when I visited at the end of November. Little did I know that I would go home much sooner than Thanksgiving.

Two weeks later at 2:30 a.m., a phone call woke me from my sleep. I answered the call and heard my brother's inconsolable voice struggle to push out the words, "Daddy died."

My daddy was gone. He had passed away unexpectedly that night as I slept comfortably 700 miles away. Literally, in a moment, my entire life changed in a way that could never be corrected.

The next two weeks blurred together—details, flowers, caskets, guests, music, peace lilies, phone calls, sympathy cards. To this day I remember the extreme heartbreak as the casket was closed and my mother, brother, sister and I stood crying in the hallway of the funeral home. Our family suddenly felt so small.

When I returned to my home to O'Fallon following my father's funeral, I saw the blue scrap of paper containing his lucky numbers and the twenty dollar bill exactly where he had placed it. Just weeks earlier, I had been amused by the tiny piece of paper that represented my father's most extravagant dreams. But time had changed the way I felt about the numbers. As I stood alone in my kitchen looking at the rows of digits, I felt a heavy sadness and regret that those numbers had no chance of ever bringing joy into my father's life, or into mine. The biggest jackpot I could ever win would not bring my daddy back—all the money in the world couldn't change that. *Money can't buy happiness.*

With sadness I took the piece of paper and its accompanying twenty dollar bill and put them inside the top drawer of my nightstand along with the bifold parchment program that had been handed out to guests at my dad's funeral.

In a superficial way my life returned to normal, but in reality, there was always an underlying emptiness. Then almost exactly a year after my father's death, my daughter was born—blue-eyed, just like my dad. Another year passed and my blue-eyed baby boy arrived. As they grew up, I often thought about how my dad would have loved them both so much. He would have surely been delighted by Savannah's beautiful spirit, and he would have been amused by little Jake's determination and frequent obstinance.

Years passed. I was so busy raising my kids that the sense of loss I experienced when my father died somewhat dissipated, and I completely forgot about the lottery numbers I had stashed in my nightstand for safekeeping.

But one day, my mind drifted back to them, and I had an irrepressible desire to find the paper and hold it in my hand. We had moved eight times in eight years, and with each move, we had packed, shipped, and unpacked the contents of our home. As I rushed through the house toward my bedroom, my anxiety swelled. I felt sick. I feared that the paper bearing my father's lucky lottery numbers would not be in the drawer—that it would be lost forever.

I fumbled through the contents like I mad woman. The funeral program had migrated to the back of the drawer. When I lifted it, I caught a glimpse of Andrew Jackson's crumpled face. And then I saw the numbers—safe and sound.

Today, that simple piece of paper is one of my most cherished keepsakes. It connects me to the things I always want to remember about my dad—that while he was a practical and hardworking man, he possessed a playful and imaginative quality, as well; that he was very satisfied with everything he had and everything he was; that he loved us all; and that he was proud of each of us.

I pay almost no attention to the lottery and have never played his numbers, even though I sometimes think I should. To me, his numbers are not lucky because I could potentially play them and win a big monetary jackpot. They are lucky to me because they represent the last thing my father gave to me—something that was in his very own handwriting; something that came from his wallet; something special to him that he secretly left for only me.

I occasionally look at the numbers and the twenty dollar bill and imagine my dad standing in my kitchen. He jots the numbers down from heart then rips the paper from the notepad. He reaches into his wallet and pulls out a twenty. He grins. He dreams. He walks out of my house.

Audrey Andersen is a self-taught fine art photographer who lives in Northwest Georgia with her husband, Bill, their two beautiful children, Savannah and Jake, and their trained therapy dog, Doodle. In her spare time, she gardens and lends her talents to helping high school seniors find and apply for scholarships and write essays for college entrance examinations. An avid fitness buff, she has logged hundreds of miles running the trails of Dellinger Park.

THE BEANIE BABIES

RACHEL BROWN

Crusty editors say don't do it. Journalism textbooks preach against it. Fellow reporters look down on peers who ignore this ethical guideline: You don't take gifts from sources.

Still, when a happily married couple in their nineties insisted on giving me two Beanie Babies out of their collection of several hundred a few years ago, I felt rude continuing to say no.

"No" was the obvious answer when a state senator wanted to pay for my room and board to come down and cover his work for a day in Atlanta. Accepting was out of the question when a manager for a park I was interviewing for an investigative story on his practices offered me a free ride on one of his attractions. Other gifts—mementos of some special story I covered—that were obviously not bribes have found their way into my life.

The little purple-brown wiener dog and mottled-tan bear I accepted from Archie and Wilma Bibbey have ridden in the back of my car ever since.

They're small, pebbly reminders of the awe I felt at getting to record this Tunnel Hill couple's—at the time—seventy-two years of marriage. As a reporter for *The Catoosa County News* in 2007, I was assigned to write a story on the couple for an issue that came out close to Valentine's Day.

If their relationship was ever more complex, it didn't show during the visit. Each one had an easy chair they passed the day in—when they weren't working in their backyard garden, canning tomatoes, or doing other work. They celebrated every wedding anniversary with a pack of Fig Newtons, repeating the ritual they began on their honeymoon back when, as Archie put it, "Fig Newtons were a delicacy." They did everything together.

I asked Wilma why she loved her husband, but she just said she didn't know.

"I just love him. I know that, and that's all," she said.

She wasn't being evasive. She just didn't feel that she needed any sort of deep, complex reason for giving her love—and why should she? Perhaps that lesson has been lost on us or forgotten—this idea that love is not something that is earned or deserved but rather a gift that is freely bestowed—just like the Beanie Babies the couple insisted on giving to me.

I didn't particularly want to take them at first. Stuffed animals, knick knacks and other trinkets have never been in short supply for me. Yet the couple kept telling me to pick out a couple to take for myself. Many of them weren't Beanie Babies they bought, but toys their friends and family had given to them. They had hundreds of them, and they appeared to be all over the house. Finally, they selected a couple of the little animals for me and told me to take them.

The weiner dog found a new home in one corner of the back of my car near the windshield, and the bear made a den in the opposite corner, each one greeting the vehicles behind me anywhere I drive. The Beanies were in the car with me when I got in a wreck in 2009, one that put my car in the shop for a month, nearly totaling it. Once my car was repaired, they went right back in their *seats* in the back.

I did not write about the Beanie Baby collection in the Valentine's Day story I wrote on this couple in 2007 for *The Catoosa County News*. I never had occasion to visit the couple again, nor was I assigned to write any other stories about them, but their story has never left me.

There were plenty of other gifts and offers of gifts that came my way both before and after, but none have left the depth of impression in my mind that these Beanie Babies did.

They're not just mementos of this couple's story. They're reminders of the love the Bibbey's shared, the love my parents have for each other, the dedication both my sets of grandparents had to support each other through good times and bad, and the fact that love—the deepest love—is often the simplest.

Rachel Brown is a reporter who has written for several newspapers in Northwest Georgia.

GRANDPA'S POCKET WATCH

DICK AFT

He hated to travel—trains, cars, ships, even planes—it didn't make any difference. Taking out his pocket watch, he opened the case and looked through the cloudy crystal at the cracked porcelain face and hands too fractured to move. He must have judged that there was enough time to tell me why he hated to travel—*again*.

My grandfather often told me about the two trips that he took that resulted in his desire to stay put. He never failed to look at his watch before he began. The time never changed. Neither did his story.

The first trip was a bad one that had a terrible ending. The last was a terrible trip with a happy ending.

Grandpa was the youngest of six sons of a German-Polish farm family. Custom followed that at age thirteen, each was given a piece of the land to farm and live on. But, there was only enough land to divide among five sons, leaving Grandpa at home with his parents. In keeping with practices during the late 19th century, male teenagers who lived with their parents were subject to conscription by the closest army. At age fourteen, Grandpa began his first trip. It was to last for a full year.

Czarist soldiers were transported on freight trains when loads were light. While it was uncomfortable, sitting on an open flatcar was better than marching. But, the ride was short. Tracks ended as the rolling countryside became boulder-strewn terrain. Walking first toward St. Petersburg, then changing direction toward Moscow was far more difficult than my grandfather's life on the farm. The best food was stolen. The best beds were sheltered.

Grandpa's only choice each day was deciding which fellow soldier with whom to talk while awaiting orders to march, stop, sleep or wake. One day, the young man he chose carried a pocket watch. The two soldiers enjoyed a subject available to very few of their colleagues—*the time*—hours, minutes, even seconds to measure the time until food or rest, nightfall or daybreak.

How strange it was, Grandpa would recall, to have but one decision to make each day. But thinking about other decisions, that was another matter.

Grandpa was sure that his army future would involve fighting, perhaps dying under orders. The trip had been a bad one and he feared the terrible ending. So he, along with the boy who carried the pocket watch, planned another trip—*away*.

Desertion from the Czar's army was not unusual. If you were caught, you didn't return. It was not the army's practice to bury the dead. So, for Grandpa, conversations of the next trip were fantasies to fill the fearful, but measurable, hours of walking and waiting. The two occupied their time by whispering about the next trip.

GRANDPA'S POCKET WATCH

Everyone had heard of America. Everyone knew of people who had found the streets paved with gold and the freedom to choose a life. The next trip would be wonderful—to America—if he lived that long.

He almost didn't. West of Moscow, he and his fellow soldiers were told to form a line across a shallow portion of the Berezina River in the western part of the Russian Empire that today is known as Belarus. Grandpa didn't know the name of the river then. Nor, did he know that he would engage in a battle with soldiers of the revolution at a place where the Russian army defeated Napoleon nearly one hundred years earlier. The generals of Grandpa's army must have known, however.

The battle lasted less than an hour. The Czarist army was much larger and better armed than their opponents. Their revolutionist opponents made decisions—to retreat, to run, to live. Most of the Polish-German Russian soldiers, didn't. Many died, including the boy with whom Grandpa had shared the time. Near his body, Grandpa found the pocket watch, open and broken.

In the confusion following the Berezina River battle of 1909, recorded only in the history of my grandfather's family, he left the army. He left with a watch in his pocket. Taking the time piece from the body of his friend was all he could do to carry out his friend's part of their dream.

He traveled again, but this time with fear of being captured and killed and with unfathomable hunger and pain. Using his rail traveling experience, he made his way to Danzig, now Gdansk, to survive a rough and overcrowded sailing to America—a happy ending.

Unlike my grandfather, I love to travel. Like him, I count the hours on an old pocket watch. I take it out of its special place. I open its case and look through the cloudy crystal at its cracked porcelain face and fractured hands. I count the hours until my next trip.

Dick Aft cherishes the memories that mementos stir in all of us. Stories, information and research accumulated during his forty years as a United Way executive are preserved in three books of United Way history—two of them written with his wife. He shares his nonprofit leadership experience as a member of a dozen boards. Applying his knowledge and a Ph.D. in Organizational Leadership and Development, he teaches, coaches and consults in classrooms, conferences and coffee shops all over the world.

GRANDMA AND GRANDPA: CUSTODY OF THE FIGURINES

PHYLLIS QUALLS FREEMAN

I folded yet another cardboard box and zip-taped the end and sides.

"*Grandma and Grandpa, here's your temporary home,*" I thought to myself. "*I must pack you away. Sorry, but Bill and I will live in only two rooms in our new place, and I hope there is a place for you. What do you expect me to do? At least I'm not giving you away. I wouldn't do that unless I couldn't care for you at all.*"

Grabbing two pieces of bubble wrap, I carefully twisted it around one and then the other beautiful porcelain figurines. Side by side, I placed them in the box of knick-knacks. They weren't just trinkets to me, though. I planned to locate just the right place for them when we got settled in our son's home.

The country figurines reminded me of my own grandmother and granddaddy—that's what I called them when they were still with us. They raised seven children, including my mother, in their three-room unpainted wood-plank house in a hollow between two mountains in Tennessee. To reach their home, we drove through a dry creek bed, turned onto the rough country path, and parked at the top of the hill. The slope wasn't too steep to walk down, past the apple orchard. Then we'd cross the tiny bridge near the smokehouse, and enter their humble home where the wooden door hung high in the doorway. When we visited, I felt it was my personal task to watch that two-inch draft space, so a snake would not slither inside. At night I cowered, completely covered by the heavy quilts piled on the soft feather bed.

Grandmother seemed to be a step ahead of her peers concerning germs and contagion in the late 1930s and 1940s. She cared for a neighbor who had tuberculosis. The only person who would enter his house, she daily delivered his lunch, changed her clothes afterward, and then washed them in a black cast iron kettle of lye soap and boiling water. Her lye soap was used frequently to clean everything in her house. "Give every plank in the floor a hundred licks," she told Anita, her youngest daughter.

When I gaze at this female figurine with the long apron, water pitcher in one hand, a basket in the other with a duck at her feet, I remember my grandmother (Amanda Jane Chandler) trudging through the field or to the springhouse, where she kept her milk and eggs cold. Her children, and later her grandchildren did chores in the field and at home. She would say, "If you aren't doing anything, you can pull weeds or sweep the yard." Yes, her partly-dirt yard with little tufts of green scattered throughout was tidy, except for fresh chicken droppings.

GRANDMA AND GRANDPA: CUSTODY OF THE FIGURINES

The thin-faced male figurine could easily be a form made from a picture of my granddaddy. He was tall and thin, and often had a pipe in one hand and a hoe in the other.

Granddaddy owed the General Store seven cents more on a purchase he'd made. He told the clerk, "I'll come back on Friday to pay you." Thomas Renzo Chandler walked about a mile and a half through wooded fields on Friday and smiled when his debt was cleared.

In his older years, Granddaddy rotated living with his children. I have Granddaddy's reddish brown double-pocket change purse. He would snap it open, pull out a quarter and send my brother to the store for a fifteen-cent loaf of bread. He'd tell Thomas, "Take a nickel and get you a candy bar."

We children loved to hear Granddaddy tell stories and especially his version of the poem *Itsy Bitsy Spider*. We'd sit ever so still because he spoke in a raspy soft voice.

So you see, after we moved to our son's home, I reached in and pulled those figurines from their box, unwound the bubble wrap, and rejoiced when I discovered they made the trip without incident. For twenty years, I've given those replicas of Grandmother and Granddaddy a home. Now they share a place of honor on our entertainment center to remind me of a simpler time.

Now, the only problem I can think of for my Grandmother and Granddaddy replicas is when I can no longer take care of them, to which grandchild will I give custody.

Phyllis Qualls Freeman is a writer and speaker who lives in Hixson, Tennessee with her husband, Bill. She crafts devotionals, human interest, and newspaper articles. She also writes Life Related Learnings *for Pathway Press, and devotionals for Reflections, Smyth & Hewlys and for Standard Publishing's Devotions. Phyllis teaches classes and workshops on emotional healing issues, and other topics. She is working on a book of stories about those who have moved through traumatic life experiences and come to a place of peace.*

DOWNED BIRD

JOANNE CROCKETT LEWIS

It peeked up at me from its hiding place in the dirt and grass stubble. I bent over and picked-up the little wooden object—a piece of dropped debris—a remnant of our local historical society's rummage sale. It was a dried-out, wounded, hand-carved chicken about four inches tall.

Like a human face, one side looked better than the other. The left side of the little bird was missing one eye like a pirate. It had also lost a piece of its tail and had multiple gouges bitten out of its body as if it had been pecked by a rival. The right side was dirty and dry but completely unharmed.

I asked if I could purchase it.

"You want to buy *that*?" the woman asked with a tone inferring she thought my request was foolish or crazy.

"Yes, how much?"

"Just take it," the woman said. "It has no value. We were going to throw it away, so no payment is necessary."

I carried it home—my mind set on reviving the little bird. I washed it, dried it, and rubbed it with multiple doses of lemon oil. I polished it like it was a precious gemstone. With each stroke, the dull brown surface soaked-in the oil revealing rich, beautiful wood grains. Soon, a dark chocolate color appeared.

My desire to know the history of the little object was strong, but even stronger was my desire to save the bird and have it start a new life with me among my most treasured possessions. And as I continued to breathe life into the little figurine, my affection for it grew.

Old objects fascinate me in that they have histories. Their histories often start before our beginnings and possibly go on well beyond our ends. In essence, they outlive us.

When we collect things—a cup, a book, a wooden chicken—we rescue them from oblivion, which to me is a stronger motivator to collect than the mere desire to own the pieces I buy. The fulfillment is not in the act of purchasing an item, but in the salvation.

The feeling I am preserving a piece of the past fills me with great pleasure and satisfaction. Maybe I am looking for the echoes of a refinement that existed in earlier times that have languished in today's world—a sentiment that I believe all generations have felt about the world in which they lived.

I turned the little brown bird upside down to record the date and place our history together began. I wrote, "Crown Gardens and Archives 10-31-09," on the underside of its base, turned it upright, then carefully placed it on a shelf on top of a vintage, glass rabbit mold. This arrangement gave the two animals the whimsical appearance of two circus animals performing an act.

The placement made me smile that day. Indeed, I smile every time I look at the little chicken—my heart growing fonder and fonder. It is a favorite of mine now.

I'll never know why the little brown bird spoke to me that day in October. I'll never understand why I selected the tattered figurine that had been so callously discarded in the grass—deemed worthless and destined for a landfill. And perhaps there is nothing to understand.

Maybe the answer is a simple one—that the encounter with the bird was no more than the chance meeting of two friends, and like friends, one does not belong *to* the other, but *with* each other.

Did I save the little bird, or did the little bird save me? I wonder sometimes, as I smile up at it riding the glass rabbit like a cowboy. Perhaps we saved each other.

Joanne Lewis is a Mary Washington College graduate with a Bachelor of Arts in history. She taught fifth grade, sixth grade and high school history. She is chairman of the Blunt House, a property of the Whitfield-Murray Historical Society, and chairman of the City of Dalton's Historic Preservation Commission. She is a collector of stray dogs and cats, linens, china, silver, decorative objects and art.

MY GRANDMA'S UGLY QUILTS

BARBARA TUCKER

My grandmother, Josie Vanover Fraley Rose, was the kind of character one reads about in an Appalachian novel—although I doubt she ever read a novel in her life. A survivor of the Spanish Flu epidemic, the Depression, and two World Wars; a survivor of the loss of three of her children, the loss at twenty-three of her husband and father of her three young children, and of her home by fire; a survivor of her second husband's infidelity and imprisonment for several years.

I have a few mementoes about my singular grandmother. One is a recording, converted to DVD, of her singing and telling stories, something she pretended to dislike but actually relished. Another is a cornbread skillet. But the most meaningful is a quilt.

MY GRANDMA'S UGLY QUILTS

It is an ugly quilt. It is made of patches of old, garish polyester garments from the 1960s and 1970s. There is no discernible pattern other than squares. It is not really quilted, but *tied*—the easy way to make quilts. It is warm and usable but extremely heavy (the batting is an old blanket) and not something I would want to display. But it means a great deal to me because it reminds me to two of my favorite pieces of literature, it makes up for what I didn't get, and it symbolizes the utility of my grandmother's life.

As a college professor in a Humanities Department, I occasionally teach English and by default have to know some literature. Living in the South, that's where I start. Alice Walker, the African-American writer, has written what I consider the best short story in the world, "Everyday Use." It's the compelling, funny, and touching story of three women, Dee (who wants to be called Wangero), Maggie (her sister), and Mama (obviously, the two sisters' mother). Maggie and Mama still live on the farm in the Georgia countryside. They kill hogs, make quilts, and sweep the dirt in the front yard. Dee, the talented, worldly sister, left home to go to the city and to college. In the story, she has now returned for a visit, but she is more interested in things than in people.

Dee has become aware of her African roots and her family's past, and she wants the churn, the quilts, and other items from her old home so that she can display them in her city apartment to impress her friends. Mama does not want to give Dee these things; they are needed for their lives, not merely artistic pieces. Dee gets into a tussle with Maggie over the quilts, and Maggie—disabled, shy, untutored—hands them over.

"It's all right," she defends her decision. "I can make more. I know how to."

In this short story Alice Walker, mostly known for *The Color Purple*, has revealed many truths, but the one that remains with me is that the knowledge *to make* matters more than the things made.

A similar theme, the conflict between possessions and what they mean, is explored in Eudora Welty's *The Optimist Daughter*. The main character, Laurel McElva, faces the sudden death of her father. Her father's vulgar second wife of two years, Fay, is one of those people who refuses to grant anything to her stepdaughter, and they get into a conflict over a breadboard that belonged to Laurel's mother. Laurel gives in, realizing she doesn't need the board to remember her mother, even though she wants it badly. The letting go moves her on to grieve her parents as people.

So, back to Josie Rose, the real, nonfictional character who lived to be ninety-eight in McClure, Virginia, who died in 2005, and who left me a quilt, a skillet, and a DVD. What I had really wanted of my grandmother's was her treadle sewing machine. It was a beauty, and one she used, not one that sat around her house for show. She used it to make those ugly, heavy, tied, polyester quilts—and she made many of them. On one visit to Grandma's when she was already in her nineties, I noticed the sewing machine was gone.

"Where's the old sewing machine?" I whispered to my mother, who was taking care of Grandma for an extended time.

"She gave it to Vivian."

"Oh, man, I really wanted that sewing machine. I thought I told you that," I responded, as if my mother or grandmother owed me the antique and as if my mother's job was to procure it for me. But Vivian deserved it. Vivian is Grandma's step-granddaughter who lived nearby and actually helped Grandma for many years. Despite the direct genetic connection, I couldn't argue. Even though I was the only daughter of her only daughter, I didn't deserve the sewing machine. In retrospect, I sounded like a teenager rather than a middle-aged woman.

What did I get? I got the quilt made on the machine rather than the machine. I got the warm covering that my grandmother pieced and tied herself. I got my grandmother's interest in quilts and her desire to make them. Mine are only a tad more creative than hers, but I think of her when I work on them. I got my grandmother's practical nature, her knowledge that everyday things can be useful and pretty and their usefulness is a testament to living. I hope I have my grandmother's strength in adversity.

My keepsake is my grandma's ugly quilt that spreads on my son's bed and keeps him warm in the winter, and I hope that he will have a daughter someday. I will tell her about why the ugly quilt matters decades later.

Barbara G. Tucker's many roles include mother, wife, college professor, novelist, doctoral student, rescue dog owner, gardener, quilter-in-absentia, lay teacher, and resident of Catoosa County, Georgia. She is the author of four novels; three published by OakTara, Traveling Through, Cross Road, *and* Legacy, *and one ebook,* The Christmas Visitors.

MY MOTHER'S GUITAR

BOB WRIGHT

My passion for music grew from listening to my family play instruments and sing from the time I was a small child. My mother, father, and sister played and sang as part of our normal family church life. My father led the singing portion of the church services while my mother and sister played the piano and organ. They were gospel singers of some notoriety and were considered by some to be equal to some of the best singers on the gospel circuit.

My mom and dad played a variety of instruments. Mother played piano, violin, guitar, and mandolin. My dad played guitar, banjo, and mandolin. They used to play and sing around the house several times a week between church services.

As a child, I would pick up my mother's guitar and pretend

MY MOTHER'S GUITAR

to play the way my parents did. They took the time to show me what to do and how to play, as best they could. The problem was, in their time, their music was simple and easy. The melodies were always based on three or four chords that always sounded country or gospel, in nature. So, I learned that regardless of what song they sang, I could play along if I knew the same three chords of any song.

I even had a Gene Autry diamond-studded guitar. The diamonds were not real but to me it was the best thing I could spend my time with while growing up on the family farm in middle Georgia.

My father had played for dances back in the mid to late twenties. He played for large crowds during Prohibition. He entertained me by telling stories from that time and singing some of the old melodies. I listened attentively and learned the lyrics and melodies. Today, I can play the same music he made—almost exactly the way he played them.

Back then, Dad had traded a Model A Ford automobile for his beloved 1928 Gretch Tenor Banjo. His eyes sparkled as he played it and told the story of the swap.

When mother sang with her guitar, there was always sadness and sorrow in her voice. The songs she sang were religious or had some spiritual message behind them. Many times for Mother's Day or anniversaries acknowledged by the church, she would sing and play her guitar.

She sang many songs, but two of them stand out in my mind as clearly as if she were here singing them today. One told of an elderly mother sitting alone in an old rocking chair—all her family gone on to their heavenly reward—sitting alone in that old rocking chair with no one stopping by and no one to care. The other song was a Gene Autry song *That Old Silver-haired Daddy of Mine*. Mom loved Gene Autry and Liberace. She tried to imitate them when she played guitar or piano.

Mom's 1925 Gibson guitar had a clear sound and an ebony finish. She loved things that sparkled or had angels on them so she put some plastic beads and a decal of an angel on her guitar.

She passed away in 1975, just after I returned home from a tour of military duty in Southeast Asia. I flew home at my sister's request because of the graveness of my mother's condition. She waited for me to arrive at her bedside.

"I'm here, Momma," I told her as I held her hand.

She squeezed my hand as best she could, and then the electronic monitoring of her brain function went flat. She had waited for me to come home before leaving this life for the next.

I have the guitar that she played, sang with, prayed over, cried while holding, and laughed at me about. It is a treasured heirloom that I play sometimes and remember the gentle sweet spirit who held it, and me. It is a family treasure that I will never part with, and I will always display it openly and not leave it in a case to be forgotten.

The rosewood fingerboard of that guitar has the rubbings of years of her fingers moving from one refrain to the next. I look at it sometimes and long to hear her sing just one more time.

Memories of her and my dad, singing and playing that guitar, smooth over all the other issues of family life growing up. I know that somehow she is watching over me and still gets that broad smile when I attempt to play and sing.

She told me once, "Honey, learn to play an instrument but please, don't sing!"

Sorry Mom, I still try.

Bob Wright is a retired physicist from Hewlett-Packard Company and an accomplished jazz musician. He comes from a family of farmers, Southern gospel singers, and musicians. He has played jazz in Los Angeles and currently in Atlanta. Since retiring, he has returned to school to finish the Bachelor of Music in Jazz Performance he began in 1967. He is attending Kennesaw State University. In addition to music, Bob writes poetry and is an avid hunter and outdoorsman. He is one of the staff turkey callers for Champion Custom Game Calls.

A STASH OF SHINY SILVER DOLLARS

DANA COOLEY-KEITH

I always felt I was traveling to another time and place when my family visited my great-grandfather. I called him, "Dad," and he was the only person I have ever known who lived and told stories the way he did. Dad lived in another state, and I only saw him about twice a year, but those were some of the most anticipated trips of my lifetime.

His way of life was very simple and fascinating to me, even at a very young age. He had no telephone and lived isolated on a large farm with cows, chickens, a fresh-water deep well, and an outhouse. I was intrigued—*haunted*, actually—by the outhouse. As we turned on the long dirt road approaching Dad's house, I would nervously announce, "I have to use the

A STASH OF SHINY SILVER DOLLARS

bathroom." The thought of trudging through the cow pasture to the dark, stinky outhouse made me cringe but ironically triggered my bladder to send a signal to my brain that it was *time to go*. After I grew old enough to make the trek by myself, I never actually went to the outhouse—I simply squatted behind the house and prayed that I could finish my business before anyone saw me.

Dad was not a person who showed much physical affection nor did he ever tell me that he loved me. However, the one gesture he made at the end of every trip would fill my heart with so much gratitude and love that neither words nor physical affection could have done more.

As we walked out on his old wooden porch and approached the dirt driveway, Dad reached deeply into his pocket. I remember the clinking sound that indicated that we were one second closer to receiving our treasure. My brother, Kenny, and I overflowed with excitement and anticipation. We could hardly contain ourselves. Then Dad's aged, leathery hand would reappear gripping tokens of his affection—a shiny silver dollar for me and one for Kenny.

My sister, Kristy, five years younger than me, always declined Dad's silver dollars. She explained that she preferred pennies to larger coins saying, "I like the small brown ones better than the big silver ones."

Dad would try to even the score and attempt to give Kristy a handful of pennies, but she refused and would take only one. The inequality troubled Dad, so he began giving my mother rolls of pennies to keep in her purse earmarked for Kristy.

Dad didn't own a car, and I never knew of him leaving the farm, so I wasn't sure how he got the silver dollars and the rolls of pennies. As a young girl, I thought he must have a secret stash of silver dollars hidden somewhere on his farm—adding yet another layer of interest to his life. But as I grew older, I realized that my great-grandfather went to a great deal of trouble to get those treasures for us. He must have planned well in advance of our visits—asking neighbors to carry him into town to the small community bank to get the coins.

Dad continued to give us these treasures until the day that he died. He was ninety-three years old.

I kept every silver dollar Dad gave to me, and I have obediently saved every silver dollar that I have come across as an adult. Today, I have my own secret stash of silver dollars. I keep some of them in a Gerber baby food jar cleverly disguised as a pink bunny—a gift my aunt made and gave to me when I was about twelve.

The coins remind me of Dad—*Silver Dollar Dad*—and how special my siblings and I must have been to him. I appreciate his sharing his knowledge, his love, and his kindness with us. Most of all, I thank him for teaching me that love is often found in the smallest gestures of life, and that these small gestures of love can sometimes make a big difference to a child.

Dana Cooley-Keith has dedicated her life to lifting-up people in their time of need. She is a certified addiction counselor, has worked with teen mothers at a second chance home, counseled abused women and children at a battered women's shelter, and helped the homeless get back on their feet. Dana enjoys creative endeavors such as painting and writing children's stories. She and her husband Mitch have raised two sons together. The couple lives in the rolling foothills of the Appalachians and looks forward to their next great weekend adventure.

PINK ANGEL

LOIS BALDWIN GOOD

The recreation room of the local retirement community, where Mama lives, filled-up as folks arrived. My mom, my husband, and I looked forward to spending time with my two sisters, their spouses, and families, especially since we didn't have frequent opportunities to all be together. The adults enjoyed reconnecting, and the children were quickly getting reacquainted—some sharing toys more willingly than others. Cameras snapped and flashed into action. The gathering on December 26, 2008 was our big family Christmas celebration, and laughter and anticipation permeated the room, spilling over into the kitchenette and small dining room.

Everyone had arrived except for my sister, Louie, and her family, which was not unusual. They often ran on their own time. My other sister and I had both called her on her cell phone to get an indication of how much longer they would be, but had gotten no response. The phone had most likely slipped to the bottom of her purse—the ring tone being swallowed-up by the noise of their small Volkswagen diesel car engine.

My brother-in-law, Tim, went down to Mama's apartment to get the last bag of apples. Those of us not watching the children busied ourselves in the kitchenette, setting things out on the tables, getting ready to eat. All we needed yet was for the lasagna to arrive with my sister's family. We were hungry, happy, and waiting.

Tim soon returned with the apples, but something was wrong. His face was drawn. There was no bounce to his steps as he quietly, but urgently gathered us adults into the dining room.

"There's been an accident," he said. The phone call had come while he was in Mama's apartment.

My split-second thoughts were about the inconvenience of dealing with police reports and insurance, and wondering how much of a further delay the accident would mean for them. Would someone need to go get them? Was anyone hurt?

"Phil and Louie are both dead."

I can still feel the shock—the numbing, heart-crushing jolt to my whole body upon hearing those words. I can still feel and hear the echoes of my moaning sobs wrenching and blurting out from somewhere deep, deep inside of me. No matter how many stories one has read or heard or even imagined—words are simply inadequate.

I am the youngest of three sisters. Louie (Louise) was the middle child, four years ahead of me. She knew me better than perhaps anyone else in the whole world. We grew up in Nigeria, and attended a boarding school, starting in first grade. Louie and my oldest sister, Barb, were therefore more than just sisters to me during the nine months of the school year when we were so far from our parents. Later, Louie and I shared a number of similar interests and participated in many of the same activities and organizations through high school and college.

More recently, she and Phil were co-pastors and lived only two hours south of us and Mama. They often drove-up after church on Sundays for delightful, relaxing evenings with us, returning home on their Monday day off. Louie and I excelled at being goofy together. We exaggeratingly swayed in unison while playing duet waltzes on the piano, we laughed while playing games or putting together jigsaw puzzles, and we relayed anecdotes and told jokes—which were often adventures in storytelling. We loved to talk about anything and everything. She was my cheerleader, confidante, best girlfriend, and cherished sister. She was only sixty-two years old.

The report said that weather conditions had made the highway suddenly turn dangerous, right where there are some curves and where trees shade the road. My sister and her husband's car slid on a patch of black ice, slamming headfirst into an oncoming flatbed tow truck. Both died instantly. Another fatality occurred nearby, about ten minutes later, after which authorities closed that stretch of road.

Phil and Louie's three adult children and one daughter-in-law arrived at their home the night before, from California, Washington, and Michigan, to spend a few special moments together before trying to get some sleep. In the morning, Phil and Louie left the house first. Their children headed north in the other car, just a little later, on a different road. The police notified them of the accident when they were about half-an-hour from our gathering. As they arrived, we took them into our arms.

I still have images of one niece just rocking her body back and forth while sitting cross-legged on the floor, too numb to even contemplate the death of her parents; of my eighty-year-old mom saying, "I don't think I'll ever have energy to do anything again"; of the countless phone calls we made; of young children not comprehending what was happening; of the taste being gone from food that wanted to stick in my throat; of thoughts that this kind of thing only happens to other people; of losing track of time; of realizing that Christmas will never be the same—that life will never be the same.

My sister's spirit appeared to an older friend of ours the very next day—radiant and bubbly, lingering for an extra moment or two to verify her presence. She asked our friend to let us know that she and Phil were just fine, and that they had been "taken up in love" right away. She wanted us to know that it was indescribably beautiful and loving where they were, and that we should savor the love around us.

I was never a collector of angels, and I have never liked pastel pink. However, while we were sorting through my sister and brother-in-law's belongings, a pink stained-glass angel, among my sister's things, caught my eye—and snagged my heart. Somehow, the figure reminded me that *love, healing, presence with*, and *forever* are more than mere words.

This angel now stands gracefully on a dresser, adding her glow to our home. I surrounded her with a few other unique angels I came across while volunteering at a local thrift shop. I lovingly placed three photos—one of each smiling sister with her spouse—among the band of angels.

The years bring healing; our supportive community continues to share tears, laughter, and love with us; and a pink angel speaks to me of the precious gift of life, of encouragement and assurance, and of a very special friend—my sister.

Lois Good delights in noticing and taking macro-lens photos of small wonders of nature, reads voraciously, relaxes with sudokus and jigsaw puzzles, enjoys power and leisure walking, and is a proficient daydreamer. She and husband Dave live in a small Indiana college town of only three traffic lights, but endless treasures. Their two sons, now adults and married, other family, friends, extensive travel, and music have contributed numerous magical moments to their lives.

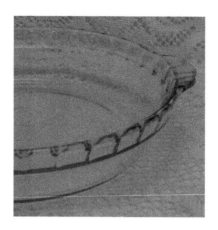

THE PIE PLATE

KAREN H. PHILLIPS

As I topped the lemon meringue pie for my mother's eightieth birthday, my eyes caught on the fluted-handled edge of the glass pie plate. It came from my late grandmother Ma's kitchen, forever filled with the fragrance of love. Before my mother made it, Ma had created this same pie, and it was her worn recipe in her own handwriting I followed.

The same glass dish had nestled chocolate pie, coconut cream pie, and steaming apple pie. The dish filled my brain with a hundred other aromas—spaghetti, mashed potatoes, candied yams, divinity candy, and spice cake with caramel icing, to name a few. The tangy smell of lemons wafted through my kitchen and carried me back to the small white frame house on Prater Road.

From my earliest memories, I associate Ma with food. In those days, it was a mom's or grandmother's best way to communicate love for her family. Though her kitchen was tiny, my brother and I loved to breakfast at the small table, which now serves as a desk in my own kitchen. Nestled in the rear corner of the house, the kitchen boasted two windows allowing sunlight to stream in and make a small space cheery. Ma made homemade biscuits, golden brown with fluffy middles, for us to heap with her milk gravy made from bacon drippings or to butter and slather with honey or red plum jam.

Family gatherings or messy recipes called for an apron, because in Ma's day, ladies did not wear anything as tacky as sweats around the house. Ma wore aprons she stitched herself, usually from a floral print or plaid fabric dominated by her favorite color, pink. Though I never wear them, I still display two of her aprons.

Standing on a chair in Ma's kitchen, I *helped* as she creamed the butter and sugar in her old Hamilton Beach mixer for a moist pound cake. I *supervised* while she and my granddad Grangie spooned out the divinity candy that had to be cooked on a dry day and tasted as sweet and pillowy as I imagined a cloud would.

My brother and I, spending nearly every Friday night of our childhood at Ma and Grangie's house, thrilled when we heard and smelled the buttermilk-and-flour-dipped fried chicken sizzling behind the kitchen's swinging door. The Colonel had nothing that compared to Ma's fried chicken, nor did he serve those freshly snapped Kentucky Wonder beans with the October bean "shellies" that Ma simmered for hours on the stove. And oh, the glorious fluff of her mashed potatoes!

Before the time of electric ice cream freezers, Grangie hand cranked the homemade fresh strawberry ice cream that Ma whipped up with smashed fresh strawberries, milk, eggs, sugar, and vanilla. We could hardly wait for the paddle to come out to scrape it with our fingers and taste the strawberry creaminess.

Everything tasted better at Ma's—even the store-bought foods. She let us sleep on her "divan," as she called the sectional sofa, with the two sections pushed together like a double bed and made up with sheets. Sometimes we got an extra sheet or blanket and made a tent over the backs, pretending we were mice. Ma brought us slices of Kraft cheese, which we nibbled from between our make-believe mice paws while we twitched our pretend whiskers and made squeaking sounds. My mom couldn't believe the same strict mother who'd raised her let my brother and me eat in the living room.

Years later, after my husband and I had adopted two babies two years apart, Ma babysat our children. She bought a little plastic table and chairs so Eric and Emily could watch their favorite TV programs while they ate lunch, and I would leave and do grocery shopping for Ma and me. Ma chopped up hot dogs for Emily and kept all Eric's favorite fruits and veggies—strawberries and carrots, for instance. Of course, she kept treats such as sugar cookies or their favorite candies on hand along with the more nutritious fare.

Every Thanksgiving she was able, Ma was in charge of the dressing and the candied yams, and often she contributed the pumpkin pie, too. Although she made many of her dishes from memory, I pleaded for recipes. She wrote several down for me.

"Karen," she said, as I watched the master at work, "the secret to good Southern dressing is plenty of sage and stale biscuits and cornbread. I make the biscuits and cornbread a few days ahead. The last thing you need to remember is to pour in enough chicken broth to give the consistency of cake batter."

The ingredients and instructions, still legible on a stained index card, have never failed me, and Ma's recipes have become musts on our holiday table.

THE PIE PLATE

I don't cook from scratch daily as Ma did and as my mother has for many years, but when I pull out the pie plate and recreate Ma's lemon meringue, apple, chocolate, or coconut pies, I see her silvery head nodding in approval. I hope, if my family doesn't taste the recipes exactly as Ma made them, that they taste the love I experienced in every dish she ever made.

In 2006, Karen H. Phillips rediscovered a passion: writing. Her credits range from Honorable Mention, Writer's Digest's 77th Annual Competition, *to scholarship-winning essay for Mount Hermon Christian Writers' Conference. She serves as email newsletter editor for the Chattanooga Writers Guild.*

THE MUSIC BOX

MARIAH FULTON

A round music box that fits easily in the palm of my hand sits on a shelf in my son's old room that is now occupied by my computer. Its metal casement is the color of cinnamon. The topside showcases a faded scene of a lady insect performing her morning ablutions. She perches on a rock rising from a stream, her wide wings stretching down towards the water. On a tree branch above her stands another insect who pours a pitcher of water over the bathing insect's head. A black wind-around handle is secured at the top of this picture, the knob still showing traces of its original blue.

Another sketch adorns the underside—a tea-stained sketch of a large bird whose chest is greatly expanded. He, perhaps she, holds a sheet of music before his open beak and trills the song,

THE MUSIC BOX

Morgen Kommt der Weihnachtsmann. The tune most of us know as *Twinkle, Twinkle Little Star.*

My father found this music box in rubbled but recovering Germany on his first business trip there in 1948. I chose it along with my stuffed white Persian cat to accompany me to Johns Hopkins Hospital in Baltimore during the spring of my fourth grade year. I stayed there ten days for a complete check-up following two extended illnesses. The pediatrician in charge of my case was a woman, unusual in those times, named Dr. Guile.

The first night, I was assigned to a bed in a large room with other children. My mother was not allowed to stay with me nor could I play my music box. Though I was weary from the overnight train ride, I found it difficult to sleep. I held both my cat and the box close throughout those long alone hours.

The next day, the hospital staff moved me to a private room. Mama stayed with me for a day or two, but then returned home to North Carolina to look after my brothers while my father was away on another business trip.

The morning following Mama's departure seemed endless. My only company was a book, my cat, my music box, and one of several nurses who checked my vital signs from time to time and brought in meals. In those days nurses wore crisp white uniforms, white stockings and shoes, and white stand-up hats with black ribbons that denoted their rank. I felt secure being in the hands of well-trained professionals. They gave me permission to play my music box, and in the afternoon, I repeatedly turned the little knob and sang its tune softly.

The next day I read for a while, then went with a nurse for various tests. Back again in my room I entertained myself with several turns of the music box. Suddenly I stopped, thinking that I heard a melody coming from the hall outside my room. I tiptoed to the door but saw no one. Returning to my bed I played again, and as I ended the song I heard the reply again. I knew absolutely that another music box was answering. This exchange continued for several minutes. When my tune heard no answer, I played four or five more rounds, but there was only silence.

A nurse walked in to check on me, and I inquired about the mysterious music coming from the hall.

"Did you hear another music box?" I asked.

"Yes," she said with a smile. "Our entire staff has enjoyed listening to *both* of you."

"Both?"

She told me about a young boy two doors down, Christopher Perry, who lived inside an oxygen tent. His heart was very weak, and his mother and father had chartered a plane from Melbourne, Australia to fly him to Baltimore.

The next day his parents entered my room and introduced themselves. I can still see their smiles, remember the gray dress his mother wore, her ash blonde hair that fell in curls to her shoulders, and Mr. Perry dressed in a light colored suit. Their gentle English accent was a delight.

And so I passed the days hoping from hour to hour to hear my new friend's signal. We began to improvise by playing in various rhythms, or by turning our knobs as quickly as we could, or as slowly, slowly as a tune could be plucked and still know itself. On the occasional day that no answer came, I asked the night nurse to stay a little longer before turning off the light. I wanted special time with my adult caretaker, but I also needed to ask new and troublesome questions about death.

The day that Mama returned, Christopher felt strong enough

to answer my call, and we improvised for many minutes. Mama walked down the hall to introduce herself to the Perrys, and they quickly bonded.

My departure date finally arrived, and before the nurse wheeled me to the elevator she brought Mama and me to the door of Christopher's room. I said hello and waved to him and to his parents who were standing by his bed. Through his tent window, I could see that he closely resembled his mother. As ill as he was, he smiled and lifted his small hand from the bedcovers. It held his music box.

Our families agreed to keep in touch, and for several years his sister, Jane, and I corresponded. Her letters and a large picture of Christopher are stored among decades of accumulations in my attic.

This very small music box accompanied me to college, on my five-year stay in Europe, to various states when I returned to America for good, throughout my married years, and into old age. Whenever events diverted my life from its carefully crafted flow and I felt isolated, my aging music box nudged loneliness and reminded me of the important lesson from childhood—*connection and comfort arrive in many guises.*

Mariah Fulton is a retired teacher who cares for rescue animals and travels abroad as often as possible with family and friends. She is careful to maintain ancient friendships, and when her health permits, is active in her writing group. Over the years she has volunteered with several organizations and has enjoyed her association with Metropolitan Ministries since 2008.

THE QUILL

CHRIS FOSTER

Buzzzzzz went my alarm, but instead of jumping up to the dreaded lawnmower as planned, I listened intently to the soft pattering of raindrops on the roof. There was no hurry to get up—it would be hours before the grass was dry enough to cut. Instead I rolled over, closed my eyes and nestled further into the soft down of my quilt. *"Ummmm, that's nice."* My thoughts turned from the practical to the whimsical.

I love a rainy day; I always have. The earthy smell, the pervasive *splutching* made from the different density of drops falling from the sky, the puddling and the *mud-luscious* demi-lakes created over the surface of the earth—all part of precipitation I so enjoy. The most sensual part of a rain storm is the ever-growing pattern of concentric circles generated as each droplet splashes into the tiny pools dotting the lawn. The dictionary defines concentric circles as objects that share the same center, axis or origin, with one circle inside the other, with the outer rings stretching further and further and eventually overlapping the circular patterns of other rings.

When I finally ventured out of bed, I sat at the dining room table and pondered my plan for the day. My hand reached for the porcupine quill I unpacked with my things after returning home the day before. *"A good writing instrument,"* I thought. I clipped the thicker end and dipped it into an antique inkwell I acquired years ago. I felt like a founding father about to sign the Declaration of Independence.

I scratched it over my photo album writing in careful script under a picture of the porcupine from which it came. It felt right. I dipped my quill back into the ink witnessing another circle forming, different from the puddles outside, but intriguing just the same. I liked the quill, and I decided it would have a special place in my growing collection of treasured keepsakes. Armed with this cylindrical spear, I began to capture the important memories within the circle of my experiences, the ones I want to set down for my children and grandchildren to read.

I like the idea of circles. Life isn't linear, as some would claim; at least that's not my experience. My life is the Elton John version—an endless round of which we are a part. *"From the day we arrive on the planet, and blinking, step into the sun, there's more to be seen than can ever be seen, more to do than can ever be done . . . in the circle, the circle of life."*

And that morning, I thought *"to hell with the grass,"* and began writing a memory from my circle.

My attention focused on my newly acquired keepsake—the quill.

I spent the last twenty-two years in the classroom working with high schoolers, watching them become adults and encouraging them to take responsibility for their own destiny. Together we explored global issues and looked for ways to make a difference.

I chose animal survival as my crusade. Many things in our society have caused the critical problems these animals face. I find myself a restless bystander. Reading disheartening reports about animals being driven to the brink of extinction forces me to look for ways to help reweave the fabric of diversity before it's too late. As my teaching career begins to wind down, I find myself somewhat adrift in uncharted waters, anticipating life's next revolution. While somewhat perplexed as to where to head, I find there are some fixed points in my concentricity. For example, it is no longer enough to merely take a righteous stand and throw money at the problem, instead I feel I must take the plunge into the mainstream of direct action. This is a growing need I can not ignore.

In response to this need, I have been sucked into another orbit, it's axis in Namibia, located in the desert region of southern Africa. Service here involves caring for big cats needing to be nurtured and re-released into the wild. The idea of volunteering there intrigued me for several reasons. For one, it is a very new country—only fourteen years old, and I thought it would be fun to see for myself how a new country establishes herself in today's world. Another reason for my interest is that ever since I visited my first zoo animals, I've nursed a searing need to visit Africa and see these magnificent creatures in their natural habitats. The overwhelming reason for choosing Namibia is that I needed to witness firsthand the only country in the world to have her animal population intact.

A small country only two times the size of Alaska, Namibia is modernizing using a new paradigm, making it a priority to find ways to develop economically while supporting both human and animal populations, and she is getting the job done! The description of the Eco Enkosini Project gave me a new dimension and direction. While following my concentric circles into a desert seems odd, the *wild orphans* of the Namibian sanctuary of N/a'ankuse called me to their service and this circle has been my widest one yet.

N/a'ankuse is a San (Bushman) word that means "the place where heaven meets the earth." Our N/a'ankuse is a rehabilitation center for the care of abandoned, injured, and poisoned wildlife, mostly big cats, from all parts of Africa. When these animals are healthy, they are reintroduced into their natural habitats. Their life cycles, eating, mating, and migration patterns are recorded and used by government and environmental planners to insure they can coexist with the human population as the country modernizes. The vision of N/a'ankuse's wildlife advocates is to play a proactive role in conserving their animal resource by "holding this invaluable trust for future generations." I was hooked. I volunteered to spend my summer there.

I wrote a Lilly grant asking for their support for this endeavor and Lilly handed me a check to make it happen. I got my reservations in March, and by June, I was circling over a country on a continent I knew almost nothing about.

As I disembarked from the plane and walked between two rows of armed soldiers the quarter mile to the airport into a crowded anti-room awaiting my luggage and the ritual of going through customs, I asked myself, *"What were you thinking coming here all alone!"* The panic faded as I was waved forward and searched for my driver, whose name was Abrahim. I saw a thin dark man holding a sign with my name on it. I must have been a sight after nineteen hours on a plane, and I'm sure I looked terrified. Abrahim must have seen foreigners like me hundreds of times before, and he knew instinctively what to do. He took my hand, reaching for my bags and in a soft but deep voice said "KOM, KOM" in the same way he coaxed caraculs, leopards and cheetahs to walk with him. They always obeyed, and I did too.

On the nearly two hour ride back to the farm he told me about himself and his village. He was a San Bushman who grew up tracking animals, living in the traditional way as a child and young man. He'd made the choice to become a settler about ten years ago. The San have lived in the southern part of Africa for over 22,000 years and genetic evidence suggests that they are some of the earth's oldest denizens. They have struggled to survive not due to the harsh climate of the Kalahari but rather due to the slaughter perpetrated on them by those who would modernize the traditional hunting areas.

There are nearly 38,000 San in Namibia and they have survived because their lands were not particularly attractive to settlers, at least not until diamonds and uranium were recently discovered. Many remain in the traditional life and work well with the conservation efforts to keep the animal habitats safe from civilized advances, but these are marginal people who have no protective weapons or modern knowledge that will allow them to survive against modernization for long, if they are not protected.

When we got to the camp, Abrahim led me to my tent which was called, "Eland" (all the tents were named after animals) and I asked him where he came from, expecting a name of a village. Instead he pointed to the sign outside my dwelling and said, "From her."

I looked puzzled and he went on to explain: "Like all San, I was created by Cagn, who created all the world and the moon. The moon laid the eggs that fill the sky, stars you call them. Cagn married Coti and she gave birth to the eland, but one day her sons killed the eland. Cagn was furious. To appease his anger and spare her sons, Coti created our people, but that wasn't enough. Cagn ordered Coti to mix the blood of the dead eland with the fat from her heart. Coti did as ordered and dumped the mixture onto the ground. Cagn sprinkled the mixture with the sacred gift of porcupine quills, and it turned into a great herd of eland. This is how Coti feeds our people and so Cagn lets us live."

This wasn't the only story Abrahim told me. One day while we were doing game count, he took me to a narrow cave near the waterhole and showed me an ancient rock painting showing the San dancing with the eland. He also showed me many animal tracks on our daily walks up the mountain sides with Medusa, the caracul. Being appalled at my poor eyesight, he set out to teach me how to find animals as they hid in the myriad of scrubby bushes and thorn trees that covered our hill and valley. He wouldn't let me go home until I could point out the five zebra on my right or tell him how many female and male hartebeests were in the herd of over forty creatures we'd see at dusk.

Bushmen have very keen eyesight and love their animals. When they kill them they dance and sing in honor of those who have to be hunted for food. They do not kill for sport or trophies, and use every part of the animal. He reported liking oryx meat best and hartebeest the least. He assured me that warthogs were tasty and must be tolerated even though they tore up our fences and trapped me in the shower. He said zebra were evil as they were lazy, stubborn and often vicious for no reason. He did however, admit that they are useful because they can find water and will dig up to three meters to bring it to the surface. Most of all he loved the big cats and spent hours studying their ways. He was fond of the ostrich too. The San use the eggshells to carry water and spend their evening cutting the broken shells into tiny circles and sanding them into flat button beads to string for necklaces and bracelets. But he steadfastly maintains that the ostrich is foolish.

My favorite San legend was one Abrahim told about Ostrich and Tortoise:

Ostrich is a vain creature, always bragging about his endurance and speed. Day after day, the animals listened to his boasting until one day Tortoise said, "It takes more than bragging to be the best." Ostrich sneered and challenged Tortoise to race him the whole length of the Okavango River and finish before the end of three days. Tortoise repeated the terms of the challenge, saying, "In order to win this challenge I will have to be at the end of the Okavango River in three days, and get there before you do." That's correct," answered Ostrich.

Off they went. Ostrich went full force that first day and that night slept so soundly he didn't wake up as Tortoise passed him. He was furious when he heard that he was behind. He ran his hardest, trampling Tortoise into the ground right into the night hole of Warthog. Warthog awakened from his sleep, demanded to know what was going on, and snorted his disdain for Ostrich. "Hop on, old one," and curling his tail over Tortoise, perched on his razor back, Warthog headed off full speed ahead passing Ostrich. Ostrich saw what was happening and laughed at Warthog, boasting that he was faster than any four footed pig. Ostrich doubled his speed the next day and easily overtook Tortoise and spent the next night drinking, bragging to his friends, and making crude jokes at Tortoise's expense. Ostrich was nearly at river's end, but said he'd wait for Tortoise to get into sight and then beat him at just the last minute just to ensure that Tortoise knew who was truly the best.

By the end of the day the tortoise was so tired that he could hardly move, but he kept on. Just before dawn he was about to give up when Cheetah grabbed him, hoping for a quick snack. But when she saw how tired and dusty Tortoise was, she asked what he was doing. Tortoise explained about the race and Cheetah sniffed indignantly, "Loud mouth Ostrich, he need not feel so smug." She flipped Tortoise on her back, stretched out her long body and, using her legendary speed, easily flew by the drunken Ostrich, who had passed out. When Ostrich awoke, Tortoise was basking in the winners circle.

"No fair!" whined angry Ostrich to the jeering of the crowd.

"What's not fair?" asked Cagn, rightly pointing out, "Tortoise won the right way, a group working together will always beat one who is foolish enough to think he can do it by himself."

The story sums up the philosophy of the San and is the key to their survival.

N/a'ankuse is owned by native Namibians, Rudy and Marlice VanVuuren, who grew up with the San and are raising their own children in both cultures. They are staunch animal protectors, but taught me that it isn't enough to protect just animals. Real stewardship means protecting the indigenous people who know how to coexist with the animals without disturbing the circle of life, and learning from them the lessons we've forgotten.

I spent a month in N/a'ankuse, living in a tent, sweating during the day and freezing at night. I mixed almost 1,000 pounds of mealy-pop with eighty crates of oranges to feed numerous animals. I nursed zebra babies, slept with baby baboons, cut up and tossed over one hundred carcasses to our big cats and chopped two bushels of apples and carrots for our two porcupines during my stay. I walked caraculs daily, coaxed cheetahs to exercise and freed one leopard into the wild. I spent about a hundred hours patrolling the enclosures at night looking for poachers. I volunteered a week at the Lifeline medical clinic for the San people. I toured Etosha, Namibia's largest national park, on a photo safari, and caught Africa's big five with ease. I baked in the sand at their plush beach resort and toured a legendary salt mine that dated back to Biblical times. I ached, cried, lived with people from all over the world who shared my passion for animals, ate very well indeed, and laughed more than I have in years. It was the adventure of a lifetime. I hope someday my path will circle back, but it may not, as I left my hiking boots for Abrahim.

The night Abrahim took me to the airport he asked me about the farms in America. Namibian farms are filled with scrubby bushes with killer thorns. The fields are not cleared, and animals roam at will, poking their heads up from time to time. I told him that he would be surprised at how we clear all our cropland and have animals in feed lots or grazing pens. I explained that most of our corn isn't made into mealy pop but goes to feed our animals directly.

"What kind of animals do you raise in America," he asked. I told him he would see hundreds of cows grazing, and feedlots filled with snorting pigs. "You would also see some herds of horses and sheep. You won't see many large herds of goats in most areas," I reported.

"No goats, oya!?" He sounded astonished and added "and I thought America was a rich country. You should go home and buy lots of goats to take care of you." Perhaps good advice.

When we got to the airport Abrahim unloaded my luggage, gave me a hug and placed a gift in my hand. The San don't put much value on material things, but do treasure giving gifts from the heart. Their gifts often have a sacred meaning. His gift to me was a long thick quill from one of our porcupines. They are sacred animals to the San. They use the quills for decorating their clothing, grind them into folk medicines, make jewelry from them, and the elders make quill pens to record their accounts and draw pictures on their leather items. They record the only information that is important to these ancient people. Abrahim's final words to me as he gently placed the quill in my hand were, "Use this to tell your children about us and what we are doing here. Make them love us, like you do. Promise?"

As I dip my quill into the inkwell, the shiny black circles forming around the tip, surround a promise that is my privilege to keep.

Chris Foster is a high school English/History teacher and an environmental activist championing stewardship practices that aid animal survival. A family farmer for nearly twenty years, Chris also worked as an environmental advocate with the Illinois South Project during the "farm crisis" of the 1980s. For the past twenty-five years she has worked to educate a generation of high schoolers to care about the issues that have the potential to make our world a better place. Building community is the most important lesson she teaches. An Indiana Master Naturalist, she spent a summer in Namibia, Africa working at N/a'ankuse, an animal rescue and release center. Mother of two daughters and grandmother of five, Chris is looking forward to retirement and continuing to pursue ways to meet the challenges of finding and promoting sustainable initiatives for our global community.

THE OLD SINGER SEWING MACHINE

AMBER LANIER NAGLE

For years, an old, weathered Singer sewing machine rested in an out-of-the-way corner in my breakfast room collecting a thick layer of dust. The ancient machine belonged to my grandmother, Margaret Mae Lanier Lanier—yes, she was a Lanier before she married my Papa Lanier, and yes, they were *distantly* related although Grandmother always contended that they were not. My great grandparents, Thomas and Deborah Lanier, gave the sewing machine to my grandparents as a wedding gift in 1922.

Throughout her eighty-seven-year life, Grandmother used the foot treadle-powered sewing machine to make clothing and quilts from flour sacks and fabrics purchased at a dime store in

THE OLD SINGER SEWING MACHINE

downtown Metter—a Mayberry-like town just an hour's drive from Savannah. When she died, her belongings were divided and dispatched to the survivors of the family. The sewing machine moved to my house that year to collect cobwebs and support a terra cotta planter brimming with Christmas cacti. I also inherited a rocking chair and a tattered quilt she constructed with her tired, wrinkled hands.

The sewing machine serves as a reminder of my Grandmother Lanier, and I suppose that's what family heirlooms and keepsakes are for—to help us remember.

She was a God-fearing woman who regularly sent money to TV evangelists so they would pray for her and her family; a superstitious woman who proclaimed, "Someone's coming to see us today," when her nose itched; a wiry woman with super human strength who only knew two speeds—*fast and faster*. She could hoe a row of zinnias, sweep a porch, and rake a yard of leaves faster than any other living being I've known in my lifetime.

When I was a child, I often slept wedged between Grandmother and Aunt Colleen in a double bed—the three of us packed like sardines under a mound of colorful quilts. It was impossible to turn over. Indeed, I'm amazed I didn't suffocate during one of my family's visits.

Her bathroom always smelled like Pine-Sol, which even today, I associate with cleanliness. As for her, Grandmother always smelled like pressed face powder and hairspray. She always wore a homemade apron with roomy pockets and a dark hairnet on her head, which she pulled down low on her forehead so that the elastic band rested in a deep, horizontal wrinkle above her eye brows.

Though I thought she was a bit odd, I always recognized what a tough, resilient woman my Grandmother was—as were all South Georgia farming wives who raised children during the Great Depression. From sun up to sun down, she cooked, cleaned, picked-up pecans, shelled peas, shucked corn, worked in the fields, scaled fish, canned vegetables, tended to five children, and *sewed*.

All women in my grandmother's heyday sewed. They gathered together at sewing circles to work on shared or individual sewing projects. They worked. They talked. They shared experiences. For women in Grandmother's era, sewing circles were much like group therapy sessions with the end result being handcrafted clothing, intricately designed quilts, and perhaps, *inner peace.*

I can't tell you how many times I've looked at that old sewing machine and imagined Grandmother hunched over it building a quilt—her foot pumping up and down to make each stitch.

Yes, that sewing machine reminds me of Miss Maggie, as she was called by neighbors, but it also takes me back to my own journey to learn to sew.

Just down the Wiregrass road a bit from Grandmother Lanier's house, my other grandmother, Ona Jarrard Jarriel, sewed for her large family, too. She taught my mother the skill, and when my sister, Audrey, and I were sixteen and thirteen years old, respectively, our mother taught us how to sew.

My first sewing project was a simple garment—a wraparound skirt that fell just under my knees with no lining, buttons, or zippers. I struggled with gaining the hand-foot-eye coordination necessary to operate Mom's electric Kenmore sewing machine. Thirty years later, I remember my first handcrafted skirt as if it still hangs in my closet—made from a medium-weight cotton fabric printed with earth-tone flowers and muted greenery. I was so proud of my first creation that I actually had my eighth grade school photo made, wearing it.

After Audrey and I learned to sew, Mom announced she would purchase all materials if we actually made our own garments. It was a clever scheme on her part to actually encourage us to sew more and eventually master the skill. We were happy with the arrangement because the more we sewed, the more clothes we had to wear to school, and Mom was happy because we were learning to sew quickly and with great precision.

We spent many Saturday mornings at the fabric store flipping through oversized pattern books—Vogue, McCall's, Butterick, and Simplicity. Selecting a style was easy. Choosing the fabric was much harder. We roamed through the aisles of the store like the wild animals of the Serengeti looking and touching hundreds of bolts of fabric considering the fabric's appearance, texture, laundering instructions, and price.

Next, we carried the bolts of fabric to the cutting table where Ms. Louise cut the fabrics to size for our particular pattern. My mom, sparing no opportunity to teach us practical knowledge, often quizzed us, "Okay girls, if the jacket requires two and a fourth yards and the skirt requires two and a third yards, how much fabric do we need to purchase?" My sister and I became very comfortable manipulating fractions in our heads.

Finally, we chose the necessary notions, paid the cashier, and returned home to start our projects. We spread the fabric out on the green linoleum flooring that lined our family room, pinned the trimmed pattern pieces to the fabric in the correct orientation, and cut.

When we got stuck, Mom intervened. Sewing can be an extremely frustrating and painful experience, at times. It often brought my mild-mannered, even-tempered, mother to the verge of a nervous breakdown.

"You son-of-a-bitch!" she would yell at the sewing machine at times, before using a seam ripper to disassemble a large tangled mass of thread on the underside of a garment. Hours of sewing left her back throbbing and her eyes strained, but it was a labor of love, worth the agony. She truly loved the satisfaction of creating something beautiful from bits and pieces of fabric, and she loved passing the skill on to us.

So, all of these memories flood my mind when I look at the ancient sewing machine—my Grandmother Lanier, our trips to the fabric store, my first wrap-around skirt, and my mother's sewing outbursts.

Time had not been kind to the old machine. The scorching heat and humidity of Southeast Georgia had taken a great toll before it was moved to my house. The wood had faded and buckled on top. The metal base had rusted. Trim pieces were missing.

But still, the sewing machine's inner beauty prevailed. The foot treadle boasted an interesting honeycomb pattern, and the base cradled four little drawers that must have hidden all sorts of bobbins, spools, and needles in a time long since passed. My eyes often gravitated to a tiny keyhole in the center, and I wondered why anyone would need to lock a sewing machine.

"I need to get Grandmother's sewing machine restored," I often sighed and said aloud, but for years, I did nothing.

My procrastination ended last year when I hauled the antique to a furniture restorer who specialized in repairing old sewing machines. Mr. Maddox, with his gray, finely groomed handlebar mustache, helped me unload the piece. He removed a silver plate under the pressure foot and plucked out a bobbin wound tightly with red thread. He handed it to me with a motion more like he was presenting me with a rose bouquet.

I pulled a small length of the crimson thread between my fingers, realizing that I was touching one of the last threads my grandmother used to construct her pillows, dresses, and quilts. It was as if I were touching her again.

I picked-up the sewing machine three weeks later. The ninety-year-old heirloom had been resurrected into a glorious showpiece—full of history, full of memories, and full of life and beauty again. I proudly brought it home and positioned it in a very prominent area of the dining room.

I plan to master that foot pedal, sew something for my nieces and nephews on the sewing machine, and tell them the story of its journey—what that sewing machine represents to me, who my grandmother was, and why heirlooms, keepsakes, and family stories are so important. They may not care, but then again, maybe it will help them see value in our ancestors and the lost arts of the past. And who knows—maybe they will learn something about me in the process.

Amber Lanier Nagle is the curator of many heirlooms and keepsakes and the brainchild behind Project Keepsake. She is freelance writer specializing in prescriptive nonfiction pieces. Her articles have appeared in Grit, Mother Earth News, Georgia Magazine, Chatter, Get Out Chattanooga, Savannah Magazine, *and many others. She is the author of an eBook,* Southern Exposure: A Few Random, Rambling Retrospective Pieces of My Life *and teaches memoir writing and freelancing workshops throughout Northwest Georgia for writers of all skill levels. Connect with Amber at www.AmberNagle.com.*

MY GRANDMOTHER'S PILL BOX HAT

PAULINE MELTON

I never met my grandmother and neither did my mother. My grandmother died, as many women who lived in the rural South did in in the early 1930s, during childbirth. The miracle that gave life to my mom, and ultimately made my life possible, was etched against the backdrop of tragedy.

I can only imagine the challenges my mother faced as she grew up without the benefit or kindness of a mother's love and nurturing hand. Life was difficult in the remote mountains of Northwest Georgia during the Great Depression and my mom was passed from aunt to uncle, sister to cousin and throughout the extended family during most of her childhood. Her father—my grandfather—was a laborer, marble miner and jack of many trades. His world allowed little time for a motherless child, and he possessed few skills to raise a daughter.

My mother's childhood was short and her life, like many who struggled to find footing in the Appalachians, was difficult. It was, however, characterized by a spirit that was defined by quiet grace, kindness, and love.

Shortly before my tenth birthday, I asked my mother about a photograph of a young woman that Mom kept on a small table next to her bed.

"Who's that?" I probed.

My mom who, by that time, was a good deal older than the smiling eighteen year old in the photograph, looked at me seriously, then slowly turned her head, focusing her eyes on the picture.

"That beautiful woman was my mother—your grandmother," she said quietly. "That was the only photograph ever taken of her."

After a few seconds, I formed a follow-up question, "What was her name?"

My mother told me that her name was Pauline. Her words cut straight to my core, and my lips softly mouthed the words, "*My* name is Pauline."

The idea flashed through my young mind that I was looking at a picture of myself—older and prettier, but a picture of me and who I was to become.

For a moment, I wondered why I had never met this beautiful lady. I had spent long afternoons with my other grandmother—my father's mother—and in all honesty, I had never given any thought to why there wasn't another grandmother in my life. As a kid, I guess you don't really think of these things until something happens to bring the issue into focus.

I continued asking questions about her, and my mother delivered answers with a heavy, deep sadness.

"She died many, many years ago," she said. "I never knew her either."

My mother's sadness resonated with me, as I couldn't imagine life without my mother. And even at ten, it was like the feeling you get when your parents remind you that some children don't have any toys to play with. Like I said, it never entered into my mind that my mother had grown up without a mom.

For years afterward, my grandmother's photograph was a fixture in our house. When our family moved, which happened more that I'd like to remember, my grandmother's picture moved with us and provided me a sense of continuity. I knew I was home when I saw her smiling face and her irrepressible grin that shined from beneath the netting of her black, pearled, pill box hat. I allowed my imagination to run wild, thinking that my grandmother must have been a movie star or led a glamorous life, knowing that women of her day rarely had such fancy accessories. She must of have been something, or someone. She was *my* grandmother.

When I was fifteen years old, I was cleaning out a closet in our house and found a dusty hat box behind some old bedspreads. I opened it carefully to discover the very hat that I had seen so many times in the photograph. As I marveled at the hat, I imagined my grandmother carefully taking it off after a wonderful evening out, tucking it away safely until its presence was required again. I also thought about my mother and wondered if she had hidden the hat, hoping that its associated memories of loss and longing would stay neatly buried behind the blankets of her memory.

The hat was beautiful. Its black velvet curves were soft to the touch and it had a costumed bow perched on its side. The bow was a wonderful accent, with tiny pearls nestled among the sequins that bordered its wings. The fine mesh that poured gently from its crest was subtle, but added an allure to it that

MY GRANDMOTHER'S PILL BOX HAT

could only be described as elegant. I was holding a piece of history and for moment, time stood still.

I didn't know what to do. Should I share my discovery with my sister and brother? Should I talk to my mom about it? In all honesty, I wanted to try it on and see if I could be as glamorous as Miss Pauline. After a few minutes of thought, I carefully put the hat back into its box and put it back up on the shelf. We shared a secret—the hat and I—and that secret would be kept for another few years until after I married and moved out of our house. I thought about the hat over the years, but never took it from its nest upon the shelf.

In 1983, my mother passed away after a long battle with congestive heart disease. There is not a day that goes by that I don't think of her and remember our time together. She showed me so many things. She taught me how to be a woman and a lady. I also think about my grandmother, the woman that neither of us knew and how different our lives might have been had we had the opportunity. I know she would have been a tough, amazing southern lady.

From Mom's possessions, I inherited the photograph of my grandmother and the pill box hat that had hidden discretely in the closet for decades.

Every night when I get ready for bed, my grandmother's photograph wishes me a good night from my vanity, and her beautiful pearl lined black pill box hat sits on the table next to it. I do not know much about my grandmother, and I never will, but I do know this—on the day her photograph was taken, she was the most beautiful woman in the world.

Pauline Melton is a gifted artist who lives in Northwest Georgia where she enjoys the company of two wonderful cats and a cantankerous orange tom who set up residence on her front porch.

MAMA'S GOLD BANGLE BRACELET

PRISCILLA N. SHARTLE

"Mama's dead!"

For a few seconds I wasn't sure if I was dreaming or awake. I remember hearing the telephone ring and glancing at the clock on the bedside table. It was 7:30 a.m., Monday, April 1, 1991. It was my sister's voice on the other end of the line, but surely Mama wasn't dead.

"What do you mean, Mama's dead?" I asked. The telephone seemed to weigh a ton as I held it tightly to my ear.

"Well, I think she is," Lindy added.

I thought, "This is an April Fool's joke, and not a funny one."

Finally I got her to tell me that Daddy had called her and said Mama had died in her sleep. Lindy was at my parents' apartment in Baton Rouge, Louisiana. I was in Winston-Salem, North Carolina at my home.

"Have you *seen* Mama?" I asked.

Lindy replied, "No."

My frustration and fear of what she was saying began to sink in and my temper flared. I screamed into the phone, ordering my sister to go see and make sure Mama really was dead.

The tears came once I boarded the airplane headed to Baton Rouge. The flight attendants were kind and tried to console me, but I could not stop crying.

My mother was a beautiful woman who lived a tormented life of alcohol and prescription drug abuse, but she did so in a functioning manner so as to give me and my brother and sister a fairly normal life—when she wasn't drinking. The last twenty years of her life were sober and happy ones filled with love for her friends, family and grandchildren.

As far as I knew, Mama was not ill. Why would she die in her sleep, and why would she die without telling me good-bye? I was her oldest child and my questions came from my heart.

After the funeral and days of cleaning out her drawers and closet, Daddy became very possessive of Mama's personal things. He said, "Take all the costume jewelry you want, but I keep the good jewelry."

We obeyed, and Mama's jewelry sat in her red leather jewelry case for the next twenty years.

My sister eventually asked for Mama's diamond engagement ring for her daughter and Daddy said, "Yes." By then, he was in the early stages of dementia, and Lindy was his caregiver and the keeper of all their worldly goods including Mama's jewelry case.

When Daddy entered a nursing home, my brother and I travelled to Baton Rouge, and the three of us divided our parents' belongings. There was a diamond ring that belonged to Mama's mother. When my grandmother died, Mama had the ring separated into two rings. Lindy wanted the larger of the two and asked me if I wanted the smaller. I agreed. She said that since I got the smaller ring, I could have Mama's mink coat. I laughed. It is a beautiful silver mink coat with her initials monogrammed on the inside. However, I don't often find an occasion to wear a real mink coat.

But it was an elusive gold bangle bracelet that I longed for. Each year when I made the pilgrimage to my parent's home, I wanted to find and touch Mama's gold band, but I dared not go through the jewelry box. It was in my sister's bedroom, and I respected her too much to invade her privacy or go through her things. I never saw Lindy wearing it, and I gave up all hope of ever seeing it again. Still, the bracelet was more than just a piece of jewelry—to me, it was a symbol of Mama's beauty and lost love.

Young and pretty and popular, Mama was every boy's dream girl. A poster girl for *Pell Mell Magazine*, the voice of LSU, her photograph on the cover was posted all over the campus. At the time, she was in love with her high school sweetheart. They had big plans to marry, and all the world was right—until my Daddy entered the picture.

My daddy was fresh home from the war, and his best friend was in love with Mama's best friend, and the two friends set my parents up for a date. Daddy fell in love the moment he set eyes on Mama. But Mama was in love with her sweetheart. And though she was attracted to Daddy, her heart belonged to another man. Yet somehow, he persuaded her to give him a chance. Becoming the Sweetheart of Sigma Chi didn't hurt. Mama blamed her parents for making her breakup with her high school boyfriend, but I think that story became glorified over the years.

MAMA'S GOLD BANGLE BRACELET

Mama eventually married Daddy. My father was a traveling insurance salesman, and Mama stayed at home and raised the three of us. We lived from pay check to pay check. She never finished college and worked sewing uniforms for a local dress shop that sold them to the students at the Catholic schools in Baton Rouge. She became an excellent seamstress and sewed professionally and privately—even making my wedding dress.

But Mama was never really happy. I don't doubt she loved Daddy. I think her drinking, which started very soon after her third child was born, was her way of coping with post partum depression, something not yet understood in 1953.

Mama wanted beautiful things and a life of luxury and never felt good enough to get the things she desired. And all this time, Daddy continued to love and protect her and give her all that he could. The gold bangle bracelet was one of those gifts—the one she treasured most in her last years.

She never took the bracelet off until the night she died. We found it on the counter in the bathroom where she must have left it before going to bed. We also found books, magazine articles and devotionals all marked with special notations.

At the funeral, we learned she had called friend after friend, cousins, aunts, uncles, and of course her children all in the week before she died. And then I heard that she had not left her home in two months, a secret she and Daddy had kept from me and to which my sister just thought was eccentric behavior. But in the wake of her death, Lindy and I realized: Mama knew she was sick. She was sixty-two years old when she died.

Years passed, and I forgot about the bangle bracelet.

On my fiftieth birthday, I asked my husband to take me to a fancy restaurant to celebrate. My husband agreed and said we had to meet our son at a local restaurant to give him something first. We were living in Chattanooga at the time and owned our own business. Our sons were working with us, so I did not think the errand was out of the ordinary.

We stopped and he asked me if I'd run the paper in while he kept the car running. I agreed and walked in to find all my children, friends and neighbors waiting for me.

"Surprise!" they shouted. "Happy birthday!"

I started to cry.

Then, the crowd parted revealing my sister and Daddy, who had driven all day from Baton Rouge to be there for my party. And in their hands was my gift—Mama's gold bangle bracelet.

Priscilla Shartle is a contributing writer for Catoosa Life Magazine. *She is the past president of the Chattanooga Writers Guild and co-author of the* History of Signal Mountain, *(Image of America Series) published by Arcadia Publishing. Like her mother, Pris always wears the gold bangle bracelet.*

COUSIN GERALDINE'S WATCH

JUDY PETERSON

On the grayest days, I wear her watch. It makes me smile. Two wide, red, leather bands frame the timepiece. It's square face showcases whimsical numbers—colorful and stretched like a Salvador Dali painting. It's full of fun, full of fire, like my Cousin Geraldine, who wore it around her wrist in the months preceding her death.

Watches track the passage of time. Cousin Geraldine's watch divides my days into hours, my hours into minutes, and my minutes into seconds with each movement of its hands. It always has the time, and like her watch, Cousin Geraldine always had time—time for me and time for others.

Geraldine Boston was born in 1939, some twenty years before my birth. She was the only child of my dad's sister, Nell

Boston, who divorced Geraldine's father before my cousin took her first shaky steps as a toddler. And so, Geraldine was raised during the end of the Great Depression by my somewhat eccentric, overprotective aunt.

Aunt Nell believed that air conditioning was unhealthy, and so she and Cousin Geraldine spent much of the sweltering summer days rocking or swinging on the front porch, waiting for a breeze to cool them a bit. But perhaps the most peculiar of my aunt's behaviors emerged in the months before Geraldine's sweet sixteenth birthday.

"No, no, no! I don't want Geraldine driving," my aunt roared to friends and family members. "I don't want her getting hurt in a car accident, and besides, there's really no reason for her to learn how to drive any way. We get around just fine."

They lived in the Dews Pond community five miles east of Calhoun, Georgia, and they relied on friends, family, and Poag, the local taxi driver, to transport them back and forth to town. And it was true—not being able to drive and not owning a car didn't prevent them from going on their weekly excursions to Calhoun to browse around Jimmy Payne's furniture gallery, eat world famous hot dogs at Lay's Dime Store, and occasionally purchase jewelry from Tim Haney or Vincent from Calhoun Watch Shop. And so, my cousin never learned to drive.

Geraldine possessed the classic beauty of a film starlet. I've seen photographs of her in her teens and twenties, and she resembled a young, exquisite Elizabeth Taylor. Indeed, suitors pursued Geraldine voraciously. Eligible bachelors continually knocked on the door hoping to gain her favor and perhaps, lure her into going with them to church or to see a movie at the magnificent Gem Theatre in downtown. But Cousin Geraldine wasn't interested in their company.

In fact, she never married, and she never left home, opting

instead to devote her life to her mother. The two women lived together in a modest, two-bedroom, white-frame house with an expansive backyard and swings dangling from the rafters of two porches like big, chandelier earrings.

After high school, Cousin Geraldine worked for a laundry service and Georgia Tufters, where she worked long shifts for thirty-five years operating machines that produced rugs. Some might classify her positions as boring and monotonous. However, Geraldine had a gift that eludes most people—the gift of making every moment of life fun and interesting by infusing the minutes of each hour with friendly conversation and humor. She was an outgoing soul who drew people to her. Coworkers loved working alongside her because she made workdays fly by seamlessly.

And Geraldine's electric personality attracted me and all of my eighteen cousins to her, as well. We *adored* her—and my aunt—and my cousins and I loved spending time with them, especially weekend visits. Laughter filled their home. Nights were full of activities such as painting fingernails and toenails, listening to music, cooking chocolate pies, and simply sitting on the front porch and listening to them tell funny stories. Both my cousin and my aunt were master storytellers and could hold our attention for hours.

Cousin Geraldine loved jewelry and had quite a collection of pieces she kept in a jewelry box on her dresser. During my visits, she and I sat on the porch and one-by-one, she allowed me to try-on her rings, necklaces, pins, and bracelets. I loved the way the gold, diamonds, and rhinestones shimmered against my skin and clothing. Draped with Geraldine's jewels, I strutted around their house pretending to be a wealthy socialite.

On Saturday mornings, we walked up the road and bought pecan log rolls and lollipops from Stuckey's—a chain of candy and souvenir shops that beckoned to travelers driving through

Georgia. Even riding to town with my Cousin Geraldine and Aunt Nell in the taxi was a cherished treat.

My cousin and my aunt are part of my fondest childhood memories, and it is hard to think of one of them without the other. But when my Aunt Nell died, the two women who throughout my entire lifetime had been inseparable, were suddenly separated.

Geraldine struggled with my aunt's death. It changed her, in a way. By then, I was an adult juggling a career in teaching and family responsibilities, but I tried to be there for my cousin, as she had always been there for me.

As the years passed, Geraldine's health slid downhill, but she did nothing to intervene and stop the decline. She found great pleasure in smoking cigarettes, and on my visits, I often found her perched at the kitchen table with a lit cigarette in hand—a curly cue of smoke escaping from its end. Her glass ashtrays cradled mounds of ashes and dozens of butts.

No one was surprised when she was diagnosed with emphysema and COPD. She had also developed diabetes and a long list of other health problems associated with the inevitable aging process. Geraldine was still living independently, but it was becoming more and more of a concern to me and my family. We discussed her living with someone else, or possibly, moving to a nursing home, but she refused, and that was that.

Geraldine had her own plan, and she called me over to her house one afternoon to talk about it.

"I don't know how much more time I have," she said frankly. "I need some help here. Will you help me?"

"Sure," I answered without hesitation. "I would be *honored* to help you."

And I did see being my cousin's primary caregiver as an honor—a grand opportunity—to help Geraldine live out the rest of her life the way she wanted to live it.

In the months that followed our discussion, I spent a great deal of time with her, along with a small, devoted band of family members and friends. Together, we prepared her meals, gave her insulin shots, managed her finances, helped her manage her prescription medicines, and all of the tasks—big and small—that have to be done when a person's body is slowly shutting down and preparing for death.

Eventually, Geraldine's health problems became so severe that moving her to a nursing facility was the only viable option. I talked to her about it. She trusted me and reluctantly agreed with the decision.

Our visits that last year were still very special. There were times when she laughed like old times and told her funny stories to me. But during most of my visits, the conversation would turn somber as my cousin spoke of her longing to join her mother on the other side. I knew the end was approaching, and so did she.

Cousin Geraldine spent her last hour, her last minutes, and her last seconds in this world surrounded by loving family members. She calmly said goodbye and assured us all she would be okay, and after singing a few verses of *How Great Thou Art*, she slipped away from us.

Yes, on the grayest days, I wear her watch and I hear her laughter and I feel her love around me. With each tick, its hands mark the passage of perhaps the most precious of commodities. And I know when my *time* is up, I'll see my dear Cousin Geraldine again.

Judy Peterson is an educator with the Calhoun City School System in Northwest Georgia where she specializes in empowering young people with disabilities. She enjoys yoga and volunteers with both Habitat for Humanity and St. Timothy's Episcopal Church. She and her husband, Eddie, are empty-nesters since their daughter, Sally, graduated from Emory University and moved west.

TOM SENIOR'S WALLET AND CELL PHONE

TOM DURKAN

I remember November 25, 2003 like it was yesterday. It was the day my father died. It is something I think about often. His slow deterioration over the months before his passing changed me in so many ways—forcing me to look at my own life and my relationship with my own children, and reassess my own understanding of value.

My dad, Tom Senior, was a man of action—a person who was constantly in motion. His life was an energetic journey, during which he saw success, failure, and ultimately the creation of a very successful carpet manufacturing business. He never stopped moving. He never stopped pressing forward.

When I was young, he was always on his way somewhere.

TOM SENIOR'S WALLET AND CELL PHONE

Surely he struggled, though I never gave it much thought as a child. The son of a humble Irish immigrant, my dad must have felt the immense weight of responsibility—providing for a wife and five children and working tirelessly to achieve his fortune. He was a moving target, and I saw more of him walking out the door to chase his next big deal than I did his sitting on the couch in our home playing with me or my brothers and sisters.

During the last twenty-five years of his life, I had the opportunity to help him build a successful manufacturing business that first gave us employment, then security. Working together for all those years never replaced the time we didn't spend together when I was young, but it gave me the chance to know Tom Senior in a way many kids never get to know their parents—as a coworker, a boss, and a business partner. Indeed, our working relationship defined our association more than those early years and shaped my understanding of my dad and his life.

I had spent nearly twenty-four hours a day with my dad in the months before his death, and we talked about life and business, family and time—each conversation a treasure. Each day had been a gift, and the *memories*—a keepsake in their own right.

It is funny what some people keep, especially when a loved one passes. I remember my sister chose to keep my father's Movado wrist watch, and my brother didn't want anything from the estate, preferring to keep and cherish only memories.

My father didn't give much credence to sentimentality, and he wasn't a keeper of curios and trophies, so when the time came for me to select a souvenir of my dad's life, I chose to keep his wallet and his cell phone. These were the items he kept on his person every day of his life—items that were indispensable to my father, a man whose world was immediate and in the moment.

I keep his cell phone in my kitchen drawer and charge it up every now and then. It still holds his phone book and contact list—symbols of his presence and commitment to keeping in touch with everyone, all the time. I scroll through the list, noticing that more and more of the names have joined him on the other side, but I wouldn't be surprised if the phone rang and someone had a question. The phone is a reminder that we all live in the now—in real time—and destiny and change are only a phone call away.

I keep his wallet in a safe place in my home. I pick it up at least once a year and thumb through its contents. Everything is how it was during those last difficult years of his life nearly ten years ago—his driver's license and insurance cards, his corporate identification badge denoting his status as employee number one of Durkan Patterned Carpets, and even some cash. Holding it in my hand gives it immediacy and presence. This was Tom Senior's vitae, his passport, his life.

Some people might contemplate that a father's wallet represents a host of things—power, the source of a son's meager allowance, mad money for a date or maybe even a night out on the town. These same people might say a cell phone symbolizes technological sophistication or a line of communication between a man and his world—the connection between a man and his son. In my case, they were among the simple tools of a man who never slowed down and never stopped building. They are touchstones of a man in motion.

I read somewhere that in the days of the Greek and Roman Empires, a father willed his sword and shield to his son, so the son could continue his father's battles, armed with the finest tools a father could provide. Maybe Tom Senior's sword and shield were as simple as his wallet and cell phone, and perhaps these keepsakes will help me keep his memory alive and contribute, in some small way, to the continuation of his journey—and of mine.

TOM SENIOR'S WALLET AND CELL PHONE

Tom Durkan is a native of New York City. He currently resides in Dalton, Georgia where he owns and manages a residential real estate company. He divides his time between business, numerous civic and community activities, and work on his farm. He cites his greatest achievement as being the father of two great kids—T.R., twenty-four, and Samantha, twenty-two.

AUNT DORIS' RED CROSS PIN

MARY LU AFT

It's a pin, a nice one, but not just a pin—not really. It belonged to my late Aunt Doris, and it symbolized to her—and now, to me—her service during World War II.

I was an American Red Cross volunteer for over twenty years. My collection of pins gathered from my travels to many chapters and conferences, numbers over fifty, but Doris' pin is special. Today, Red Cross pins are designed to identify the chapter, region, or service they represent. Her pin is just a plain enameled red cross.

Doris' Red Cross career began in 1944 when she asked for an overseas assignment with the American National Red Cross which provided many support activities to overseas troops. A single social worker with twelve years of experience, she was motivated by her will to "do something concrete and personal in the war effort."

Her assignments placed her in various hospitals that treated the newly wounded and recovering casualties from the European Theatre. Military personnel were primarily American and British, but others came to them from other countries and memories of their homelands that had been taken over by foreign armies. Her final assignment with the Red Cross was aboard the Queen Mary, helping orient the British wives and children of American servicemen as they sailed to their new homes in America.

I was constantly reminded of her overseas duty by her ever-present 1940 maroon Ford which she had left with my father for safe-keeping. It occupied our driveway, and we were proud to tell people we were taking care of it until she returned from overseas. Periodically packages would arrive for my brother and me—usually books published on fragile war-time paper. As she was in England, the language barrier was minimal, and I proudly learned that not everyone spelled the word, "color" as I learned in the second grade. Widening my horizons was what Aunt Doris did well.

She was never allowed to disclose her exact location, but that didn't keep her from dropping hints and my parents from guessing where she was. To me, overseas was an immeasurable distance from Iowa.

Doris asked my parents to save all of her correspondence to them, and today I have all of her letters and my parents' letters to her. I especially cherish descriptions of hospital life in England where bombs were dropped nearby and civilian goods were heavily rationed, to descriptions of everyday life, stateside, in small town America where people also dealt with rationing and anxiously awaiting word from overseas that their loved ones were out of harm's way. Doris' time in England was perhaps the most exciting event in our family in those years. She and my father had lost their parents when they were quite young, so we were all the family she had.

Besides the letters, Doris wrote profusely about her experience. One hand-typed manuscript has 105,000 words—counted for the benefit of a potential publisher. Her writings were never published, but two copies and a condensed version are in my possession, and occasionally, I open the boxes and randomly read a chapter or two. It was another time, another place, but always in Aunt Doris' voice.

Twelve years after she deployed to England, she took me back with her on a nostalgic trip to Europe to visit the Paris she only saw immediately after Liberation, and the sights and friends she grew so close to in England. By then, I felt I knew many of her friends we visited, especially Margaret Holmes, in whose home we stayed for four weeks. Margaret was quite a character. She had a heart condition, and her doctor prescribed one cigarette four times a day—mostly to get her to sit down and relax.

The many British Red Cross volunteers who worked in the hospitals graciously welcomed Doris and me and proudly showed us how the twelve years since the end of the war had immeasurably improved their lives. They served copious amounts of sugar and always said that wartime rationing of sugar was one of their greatest hardships, and so they were making up for it.

There was Mrs. Salisbury, a generous lady who told me to pick anything out of her glass front cabinet for my birthday; Maude Johnston, who wore a blue porkpie hat, thick glasses and stood in the garden of her 17th century cottage surrounded by shoulder-high plants as we took her picture; the couple, Mr. and Mrs. Baker and Miss Percival and the list goes on. Each warmly, welcomed us, happy to see their American friend and her niece.

AUNT DORIS' RED CROSS PIN

That pin evokes so many memories of Doris and her overseas experiences, and I treasure it. In her own words: "Under the auspices of the American Red Cross during World War II millions of American and Britishers gave of themselves and their substance on behalf of American servicemen. In the giving, they wove a fabric of international good will." Indeed, Aunt Doris wasn't a soldier, but served, nonetheless.

Mary Lu Aft knows that communities, as well as individuals, treasure mementoes. As a community volunteer for over forty years, she has shared experiences with hundreds of others as she has learned to sell books, trained and managed volunteers and served her community. Her passions for traveling, knitting and reading, along with her life as a wife, mother and friend, have provided many stories that fill her life.

A BLESSING AROUND MY FINGER

CYNTHIA WILSON

It's tiny by today's standards. The center stone is probably only about .15 carat. But in 1965, it was the wedding ring that made my mother blush as a young bride. My dad had picked it out himself and bought it on a monthly installment plan from Sterling Jewellers surprising my mother with it. She was only twenty when she donned that ring for the first time. Young and fresh and a little on the shy side, my mother dreamed of a family of her own and of a future that was bright and new.

It was a decisive move on my dad's part that I admired.

Oh, how I relish all the stories my mother has told me through the years—about how my dad followed her around Dalton, Georgia on his motorcycle. With Marlon Brando hair and no doubt an attitude to match, my dad found the right girl for him and would not take "no" for an answer.

I've probably made my mother tell me the story a thousand times before—the one about how she didn't even like him at first and repeatedly turned down his invitations. He was young, and daresay, arrogant and had a colorful vocabulary back then. He dreamed of being James Dean or maybe Steve McQueen. But, on that fateful day, when he vroomed up beside her car, as he did everyday, there was just something about the way the sunlight fell on his face that made her think, *"If he asks me again, I might just say 'yes'."*

A brief six months later, they stood in front of the preacher and their only witness, the preacher's wife, and said "yes" to each other with their eternal vows. I'm grateful to say those vows have remained eternal to this day some forty-six years later. That little, sweet wedding ring that my dad worked so hard to produce was secured on my mother's petite finger and the newlyweds went off to begin a grand adventure together.

A few years later when I came along, they knew immediately I was the independent type. I was always writing poetry or singing or dancing or simply daydreaming for hours upon end. I was not the sort of girl to follow the grain. So when it came time to think about marriage, which seemed to come much too quickly for me, I ran in the other direction. I ran off to make an adventure of my own in the biggest city I could find—New York City.

I did have adventures as I forged a life for myself. But not everyone understood why I had to go it alone. Why not marry? Because, it just didn't seem like it was for *me*. I had worked so hard to make my own way, probably as hard as my dad had worked for that ring. And when I had burned a path so bright and hot for myself no one was more surprised than I to find that as that path cooled and became clearer, it was actually leading me back home.

So there I was, thirty-four, with a photo album full of wild adventures, but still no husband. And for the first time in my life, as I stared at the crossroads in front of me, I thought, *"Hmm, maybe I will get married someday after all."*

Well, who knew *someday* would come so quickly? One month after moving back to Georgia a cousin introduced me to the man I would marry some few short months down the road.

Now, I stood before a preacher next to my soon-to-be husband with my parents bearing witness. My mother had loaned me her very first wedding ring as my *something borrowed*. I wore it with pride that cool, October day, on my right hand. As we spoke our eternal vows, and John slipped my own wedding ring onto my left hand, I knew that nothing would ever be the same again.

John and I had a clever plan: small wedding, *big* honeymoon. I decided to wear my mother's wedding ring for the duration of our honeymoon. I kind of liked the idea of this innocent band of memories going off with us to places it had never before seen. We experienced the breathless beauty that is Paris and the warm, sensuousness that is Rome. All the while, my mother's wedding ring accompanied me and I felt a sense of calm, almost as if it were a blessing around my finger rather than simply a ring.

Back in the states, I still wore the ring and it became to me something that grew deeper in meaning as my new life progressed. Back home, close to my parents, and now able to converse with my mother as a fellow married lady, the ring took on a warm, cello-like resonance when I looked down upon it.

My mother, once the innocent and young bride, had been so kind in her wisdom to pass on her beloved first wedding ring to me. While my own wedding ring is dear to me for so very many reasons (pride, love for John, a symbol of our marriage) I still keep my mother's ring close by.

Maybe it's to remind me that I am my father's daughter for never being able to take "no" for an answer. But one lesson it took me a while to learn, (in fact it took a move across the entire eastern seaboard for me to learn) was that when I finally did say "yes," that was when my own adventure would truly begin.

Cynthia Pierce Wilson is a Georgia girl who spent fifteen years living in New York City where she enjoyed several creative outlets including the performing arts. After moving back to Georgia in 2008, Cynthia met and married her husband, John. The couple lives in Dalton where they share a love of the arts, fine food and wine, and everything French.

DAD'S DRESSER

JULIE MOSS

My father and mother met in April 1964 when both of them were in the military. They married six weeks later and had one of the greatest love affairs of all time. My parents died fifteen days apart in August of 2003. My family expected my dad to die—he had lung cancer—but my mother's death was unexpected and came before my father's. Telling my father was the worst thing I have ever had to do. He was so incapacitated that he could not attend her funeral. It was a very sad time for our family.

My dad actually went into the service twice. The first time he had to get out because his father died in a car accident, and he had to arrange for care for my grandmother who suffered from ALS. He went back in after his mother's death and immediately was sent to Vietnam for nine months. I'll never forget watching him leave from Chicago's O'Hare Airport. He looked so handsome in his dress blues. When he came back, we moved to Georgia and my father's job in the service changed. His new duties required him to travel about nine months out of the year, but although he was absent a lot, he always made up for it with plenty of family time.

I was a *Daddy's Girl*. He and I were great buddies, and I spent a lot of time with him—my hero. When my mother went to work on very long shifts, six days a week, Dad and I went on hot chocolate picnics which entailed going to a local lake park and having hot chocolate and snacks. He took me swimming at the NCO pool on the military base and on bike rides to Eckerd's Drug store to have lunch. Our Saturdays consisted of cartoon watching and breakfast, then, he summoned me outside to help him bleed the brakes on the Volkswagen he'd bought as a second car. We spent many weekend afternoons listening to records and recording them to reel to reel tapes. One day I asked him why we didn't just listen to the records, and he told me, "Recording them and listening to the tape instead, keeps the records in excellent condition."

He played guitar, harmonica and banjo and sang *Froggy Went a Courtin'* and *Hound Dog* to me.

My father was very strong and would do handstands and walk across the room for laughs. He brought back fantastic long leather whips from Vietnam and would stand in the backyard and crack them so loud, the sound echoed throughout the neighborhood.

He also enjoyed woodworking. He had a shed that he converted into a woodworking shop where he made all sorts of things. I'll never forget the smell of the freshly cut wood and stain. I have many keepsakes that my father made with his own hands including a butcher block from my mother's kitchen, a bookcase he made for me, a coffee cup tree, an old toy box I refinished to store all his old, pristine albums, and a bassinet he made for my son when he was born. Though I treasure all of the things he made, the keepsake I treasure most is an item he did not make—my father's old dresser.

My parents always struggled a bit, so it was a big deal when they bought their first bedroom furniture. The set was made out of pure oak—very heavy and ornate, but not in a feminine way. It consisted of a new king size mattress, box spring and headboard, two nightstands and two dressers. My mother's dresser was low and long with nine drawers and a mirror. My father's dresser was tall and had two doors with drawers inside and two drawers below. I remember my father standing in front of his dresser, getting ready for a night out on the town with Mom.

He eventually made two little platforms to go inside to give him more shelf and organization space. He kept all his aftershaves, colognes and jewelry inside those doors, and in the drawers were his unmentionables and old-school-style handkerchiefs, which he carried for emergencies. I thought that dresser was the best dresser ever made. It was unlike anything I had ever seen.

My father and I were on the *losing team*, as I referred to us because my sister was very close to my mother and my father always deferred to my mother. I was lucky, though because he taught me things that he didn't have time to teach my sister like changing tires and checking fluids in the car—he always emphasized the importance of maintaining vehicles. He taught me how to use a grill and cut the grass. He taught me the importance of responsibility in my personal life. He always told me how beautiful I was when I was feeling fat and ugly. He once said to me that if he was my age, and not my dad, he would love to take me out. That meant a lot to me as an awkward teenage girl.

He and my mother taught me how real love works with mutual respect and teamwork. He also taught me to be self-sufficient so I would never have to rely on a man to get things done. Once after complaining that my friends weren't around to do something, he gave me some advice I still use today, and it is the best piece of advice I ever got from my dad. He said, "Never wait on someone to do something. If you want to see a movie, go see it, don't wait on your friends because you will miss out on a lot of fun waiting around for other people."

I share his message with my son, nephew and my friends today. I never feel *funny* about doing anything by myself because of his advice.

I was lucky enough to work with my father for about a year doing store inventories. It was a great experience. During that time, I called him "John," not "Dad" because of the professional environment.

He always had his hat, a cup of coffee and a lit cigarette. One girl we worked with often, called him John Boy—how fun! I enjoyed working with him, and while I knew he was well-loved before by many people, I was able to see firsthand that he was well-liked and respected at work by coworkers. I saw that he was a positive influence to so many and a real team player.

On several occasions, store employees would ask me if I was in charge.

"Why do they keep asking me that?" I asked my dad one day.

"Because you look like you know what you are doing," he replied.

His words boosted my ego to the moon. He always knew what to say to me to build my confidence.

I never saw him angry at work. He always looked for solutions to problems—a trait I inherited from him. It makes me seem kind of butch sometimes, because I am a cutthroat problem solver, which is usually a male trait. Oh well, there are much worse things in life than seeming masculine.

Years later when my parents died, my sister and I sold the house and divided their belongings as we wanted. I made sure I got several keepsakes, but above all else, I wanted his dresser—more than the bassinet he had made with his own two hands and more than the priceless record collection that he and I enjoyed together.

Years of storing all his personal belongings in the dresser had left his "dad smell" in the wood—an imprint of him. Even now, eleven years after his death, I can still open the dresser's doors and smell my dad. I breathe it in, and it's as though he is still with me.

Julie Moss is an aspiring writer who is finishing her Bachelor of Arts in Gender Studies at Middle Georgia State College. She is a single mother of one son and is looking forward to compiling stories from her life as a former military brat, travel agent, Waffle House waitress and inventory auditor. She has lived in Georgia on and off for over thirty years and plans to relocate to Southern California in the next few years.

GRANNY ROSIE'S ORGAN AND MILKING STOOL

JESSE VAUGHN

I have two favorite keepsakes. My great-grandmother's milking stool inspires in me discipline and hard work—a reminder that others worked very hard in order that I might not have to toil as they did, and that I am not far removed from the South Carolina cotton farm of my ancestors. It sits against the wall in my office just beside my door on the way to my desk.

My other favorite keepsake is a large early 20th century pump organ that also belonged to my great-grandmother. The organ is positioned in the family room of my home and reminds me to value family, family gatherings and the time spent with the ones I love.

Both the organ and the stool are general reminders of how fortunate I have been in my life—fortunate in that three of my four great-grandmothers lived well into my formative years. Each of them was a bottomless well from which I could draw story after story. Each of these women had seen their share of good and bad. They had known happiness and heartache. Each left indelible marks on the sketch of my life, and for that, I am truly blessed.

The one I knew the least was probably the one who favored me the most, Mamie Ross Vaughn. Granny Mamie was my paternal grandfather's mother. She was married to my namesake, Jesse Lee Vaughn. Even though Jesse died young in the Great Depression, he and Mamie still had seven children who lived to adulthood and a pair of twins who died at birth.

By the time I came along in 1973, Granny Mamie was an old lady but she was so excited by my arrival. She had four sons and a multitude of grandchildren and greatgrandchildren, but my younger brother and I were the only boys in our generation. It was up to us to carry the Vaughn name into the future. So, when I was born and named for her departed husband, I achieved an unrivaled status in her eyes. While she loved my brother and my cousins very much, I always knew I held a special place in her heart.

My maternal grandfather's mother was my Ma-Maw. She was the most accomplished of the group. While Granny Mamie never ventured far from the farmland of upstate South Carolina, Ma-Maw traveled to many exotic locales. Ma-Maw, with the help of her daughters, my Great Aunt Dot and Great Aunt Clara visited every state except Alaska. When Aunt Clara and Uncle Robert retired to Florida, Ma-Maw went with them. They lived on the Indian River across from Cape Canaveral. I was fortunate to stand by my great grandmother and watch the space shuttle

GRANNY ROSIE'S ORGAN AND MILKING STOOL

fly into space. It was Ma-Maw and my Holcombe relatives who encouraged me to dare great things.

But the one I knew the longest and the best and the owner of the milking stool and organ was my paternal grandmother's mother, Granny Rosie (Rosa Mae Capel Hawkins). She was married to Elbert Rowley Hawkins and they had five children—Benjamin Franklin (B.F.), Leila Mae (my grandmother), Zebulon, Thelma, and Hugh. My Paw Paw Eb died in 1968 not long after my parents were married, so I never knew him. Mom and Dad say everyone fretted that, "Rosie wouldn't make it six months without Eb," but she sure showed them a thing or two. She attended many of the funerals of the folks who doubted her resolve before dying in 1990. Granny Rosie was as even tempered a person as you would ever meet—never getting too high or too low. She had a strong faith that she wore not for everyone to see, but to comfort and inspire those in her life.

Granny Rosie's house was always fun to visit. She had taught school before marrying Paw Paw, and somehow, she managed to save some of her money to buy the organ. It was manufactured in Ann Arbor, Michigan and shipped to the Greenville Piano and Organ Company. She bought it and had it delivered out to the farm.

The delivery of the organ was an issue of disagreement in later years between myself and my grandmother. I seemed to recall that Granny Rosie told me a story of the organ being delivered in a huge crate on the back of a mule-driven wagon. My grandmother said that Granny Rosie told her it was delivered on a Model T Ford truck. I have my doubts of my grandmother's story, but never dared to tell her I thought she was wrong.

The organ occupied one end of the large formal living room at Granny Rosie's house. Not long before Paw Paw died, they built a smaller brick house across the road from the large white clapboard farmhouse. This house had central heat and air and would be where they would live out their golden years, but Paw Paw did not make it that long.

As kids, the living room was one of those places my brother and I hated going because we had to sit still and not touch anything. Our parents would threaten us within an inch of our lives if we touched anything.

The organ was the one redeeming feature of the room. Granny got a kick out of watching us try to play it. My brother and I loved to make sound come from the old organ while pumping the pedals vigorously with our feet. It sounded more like the death throes of a stricken goose than any kind of music, but Granny would just clap her hands and laugh at our *performance.*

Granny Rosie's house also had a shed in the backyard about thirty yards from the back door. It was an odd shed because it was an A-frame. Probably not more than 8 feet high at the apex and maybe that wide at the bottom, although my memories are of it being much bigger. The two ends and the floor were made of wood and the sides and roof were made of sheet metal. She stored all kinds of implements and tools in there—things that harkened back to the days when they lived across the road in the old farm house.

I can still recall the smell of the shed. A rich combination of sawdust, rust, and fertilizer.

The story goes that my Dad and his Bridwell cousins, Ronnie and Kenneth, often locked their younger cousin, Edward in the shed, so they would not have to entertain him. Our papa, Granny's son-in-law, planted a garden behind the shed each spring. Rows of corn, green beans, tomatoes and squash grew in a little clearing behind the house and shed and beside the old

GRANNY ROSIE'S ORGAN AND MILKING STOOL

garage. I remember Papa killing a snake with a hoe and hanging its body over a tree limb, and I remember Granny hanging clothes out to dry in that area of the yard.

Most of all, I remember visiting with Granny Rosie on her screened porch. She loved to sit out there when the weather was good and find out everything we were doing back home. Since we lived three hours away, we did not get to see Granny or any of our South Carolina kinfolks as much as we wanted. When we did visit, we told Granny all about our classes at school and our football and baseball teams. We told her about church and all of the plays and performances we had been in since our last visit. She always beamed with pride and showed great interest in all of the things we did.

I begged her for stories of what her life was like back in the day. I laughed at the stories she told—of how she remembered the first car, washing machine, gas stove, airplane, and other such items. Like the child that I was, I only thought in terms of myself and how strange it was for me to envision a world without cars or TV. As I have grown up and have my own family, it amazes me just how hard folks like Granny Rosie had to work every day—mere survival was a real accomplishment.

The milking stool sat out on the screened porch along with an old sharpening stone wheel. While we talked, I sat on the stool and my daddy would put a fine edge on his pocket knife.

Granny Rosie never told us that we had gotten too dirty or that we were too loud. She just seemed to soak in everything about us. She told us anything we wanted to know, but we had to have the courage to ask. Granny had known the tough times of the Depression, wars, the loss of her husband and the loneliness that comes with living alone for over twenty years, but she always looked forward to the next good time—and she had a lot of those good times, too. Many of those were not planned or scripted. Instead they were just short visits on the porch in the cool of the evening after a hot summer day or to watch the leaves fall as autumn arrived.

And so the milking stool and the pipe organ remind me of Granny Rosie, and my other great-grandmothers, as well. And though they are relics from a different era, their lesson is timeless—*persevere*. The bad will come, and the good will too. Sit on your little wooden stool and do the work that must be done, so soon you can pump the pedals and make the pipes sing.

Jesse Vaughn describes practicing law in Calhoun, Georgia as a few parts Atticus Finch, a few parts Law and Order, *and a lot of* The Jerry Springer Show. *He has been Chairman of the Board of Directors for Habitat for Humanity of Gordon County for several years, and is an active volunteer with the Chamber of Commerce. He and his wife, Christy, have two children—Sarah Beth and Hudson. Vaughn keeps his great grandmother's milking stool in his office as a constant reminder of family ties and sacrifice saying, "We stand on the shoulders of all who went before us, and we owe our best efforts to them."*

PIECES OF ESNOMS-AU-VAL

FRANCINE FUQUA

In Esnoms-au-Val, France in the September of 1913, Jean Bourguignon sat down on an old trunk and wiped his brow. It had been a hard day, much more difficult than the usual days he spent at the armory in Langres. As captain of the infantry division, he wasn't subjected to the hours of hard training his men had to endure each day and mostly sat at a desk.

It was the last day of harvesting the acres upon acres of vineyards that surrounded his ancestral home in Burgundy. When his father died three years before, it became apparent that his mother and younger brother would not be able to carry on with the winemaking business that had been the lifeblood of the Bourguignons for centuries. So every September, he took two weeks leave to direct the harvest. That was the least he could do.

Guilt flooded his mind as he recalled the day he had told his parents that he wasn't interested in following their footsteps and carrying on the family business. His father's face had turned ashen, and his deep-set blue eyes had flashed in anger, then in pain. His parents had always known that Jean wasn't like anyone else in Esnoms-au-Val. Their son wasn't content to simply work the farm, tend to the vineyards, and help in the other family business of making wooden shoes. They knew he spent hours every evening in the church parsonage with Father Martin. The old priest, aware of Jean's sharp mind and desire to learn, had taught him to read and write at an early age, introduced him to the wonderful classics that filled the church's bookshelves. He also taught him Latin, and how to read music so he could play the church's organ on Sundays.

When Jean reached eighteen years of age, father Martin visited the Bourguignons home, and told Nicolas and Adèle Bourguignon that their eldest son was destined for great things and needed to pursue a formal education. His mother immediately assumed that Jean was going into the priesthood, and that was all right with her as she was very devout. When they learned that their son wanted to pursue a military career, they were stunned and distraught. As the elder son and following the custom of the day, he was to inherit the farm, the home, the vineyards and the family business. Jean told them he would happily give up his inheritance to his brother and only asked that his father sell a few lands to pay for his studies. The die had been cast, and he left Esnoms-au-Val for the city of Langres, trying to ignore the pain in his father's eyes. Had he known that the old man would die shortly after, he probably wouldn't have left and would have given up his dream, but it was too late. Instead he came back to Esnoms-au-Val as often as he could to help out.

Jean looked across the orchard. It was a beautiful September day. The peach, apples, and pear trees were still laden with fruit and bees buzzed all around them. Swallows dove between the walls of the barn. He could hear the cows' bells as they returned from the pastures, herded by his nephew Claude and the old family dog. Wonderful smells came out of the large home that had been their homestead since the 17th century. Jean did love the place and was grateful that Langres was not far away so that he was able to spend most of his weekends in Esnoms-au-Val.

Marie, his beloved wife, and his two children, Albert and Marguerite, loved the farm too. But Albert had followed in his footsteps and was now close to graduating from the prestigious St. Cyr Military Institute. He had not been able to visit for months.

Jean stood up and stretched his legs. Dinner would be on the table soon and he was hungry. It was time to go in. His plans for the evening were already set. He would retreat to the barn and work on the armoire he was building out of cherry trees he had cut in the grove. It was nearly finished, every piece sculpted by hand, in exquisite detail. It would be Marguerite's dowry someday. Piles of hand-embroidered linens sheets and tablecloths were already destined for the armoire's shelves. Jean smiled to himself as he entered the kitchen.

His mother grinned. "You can still smell food a mile away, can't you? Let's eat, we are going to visit the Duponts after supper. They invited us to play cards."

Jean was quick to reply. "You all go, I play enough cards at the barracks with my men. I need to finish the armoire, all I need to do is to put all the pieces together."

"You need your nephew's help for that, Jean. Those pieces of cherry wood weigh a ton. Tomorrow is Sunday and he can help after church. He is committed to the card game tonight."

Jean looked at Claude's face and realized that playing cards with the neighbors was much more fun than putting a heavy piece of furniture together especially now that a young and pretty cousin was visiting them; besides Claude had worked very hard on the harvest all day.

"I can handle the armoire by myself, dear, and my plans tomorrow afternoon are to finish writing that music piece the choir needs. I should have time to finish it before I need to return to the base."

Marguerite protested. "Papa, you promised to help me with the oil painting we started last weekend. How will I ever get as good as you if you don't help me? Father Martin says his eyes have left him and his hands tremble too much to paint."

"I only have two hands, Guite, and that oil painting isn't a priority. Next weekend, I promise."

Marie put the fragrant boeuf bourguignon and potatoes on the table and looked at her husband. "You will also need to find time to clean the yard. There are grapes skins scattered about, and the chickens are having a field day eating them. If you remember, they got drunk eating them last harvest. And Marguerite, you will have to scrub those skinny legs of yours real well. Grape juice is hard to remove. You and your friend jumped around those barrels too high while squashing the grapes the last two days. You are stained almost to your elbows."

Jean dove into the stew. Pleasing everyone during his short stay at home was difficult. He wanted his children to learn the fine things of life—music, painting, sculpting wood, all the things he excelled in. There just wasn't enough time in a day.

After supper, he went to the barn and worked for hours assembling the beautiful armoire. *"It is a showpiece,"* Jean thought to himself. *"Marguerite will enjoy it the rest of her life."*

By late evening he returned home, his back so sore he could hardly stand erect. Everyone was already fast asleep.

When Jean did not come down for breakfast the next morning, Marie went up to the bedroom and found him bent in two, excruciating pain visible on his handsome face.

"What's wrong, Jean? Come down for breakfast, it's getting cold and we need to leave for church pretty soon."

Jean's breath was labored. He grimaced as he attempted to rise. "My back is killing me, I don't believe I can make it to breakfast or church. I'm sorry."

"Yeah, and I bet I know why. I told you to leave that armoire alone until Claude could help you lift those heavy boards, but no—you never listen to me. Go ahead and lie down and rest. I doubt if you can go back to the post in this condition. Men—they never listen." She went out of the room and slammed the door.

Jean wasn't able to go back to the post and lay in bed in agony for two days. On the third day, he was burning with fever. The doctor made his weekly visit from village-to-village and Friday was his scheduled day for Esnoms-au-Val. Marie realized that she had to get him help before the end of the week and sent Claude to find the doctor and bring him to her husband's bedside.

Jean Bourguignon died on Thursday morning; he had suffered a massive kidney infection that spread poison throughout his body. He was fifty-three years old. He would never know that World War I was declared a few months later and that his son Albert would march on the Champs Elysées in Paris in celebration of Bastille Day and his graduation from St. Cyr before going to war in August 1914. Nor would he ever know that American troops commandeered several rooms of the farm in 1917, and that Marguerite would meet a handsome American officer and marry him after the war. Indeed, in 1918, young Marguerite boarded a large ship and followed her husband to Los Angeles. In the cargo of the liner were many of her father's beautiful paintings, several objects he had carved, his music book and the magnificent armoire.

In Chattanooga on a spring day in 2012, I decided that it was as good a day as any to begin my spring cleaning. I began with polishing furniture. The most difficult of all to dust and polish is that massive cherry wood armoire because it is so exquisitely sculpted. And as I always do every spring, I marvel at its beautiful craftsmanship and I get lost in the waves of memories that engulf me. My mother's grandfather, Jean Bourguignon built this armoire for his daughter, my grand-aunt Marguerite, from cherry trees he cut in his backyard. I have been to the old homestead in France many times and know every detail about this ancestor of mine. Almost one hundred years after his death, he is still legendary in Esnoms-au-Val; 'the boy who made good'— the man's whose beautiful paintings still adorn many of the village's homes.

When his daughter Marguerite passed away in 1989, she willed the family treasures she had brought to America so many years ago to my mother and me. Marguerite never knew the joy of having children and left everything to her brother Albert's heirs: his daughter Jacqueline—my mother—and myself. I had also married an American and moved to the United States in 1962, bringing my mother to America a few years later.

Great-grandfather Jean's masterpieces journeyed from France to California then to Tennessee at a high transportation cost and now have their place in my home in Chattanooga.

I have so many treasures—a photo of my great-grandmother in her ball gown, a copy of a page of music, each note hand-drawn in India ink by my great-grandfather Jean Bourguignon, and hand-carved shoes he made for his wife to go dancing. I also have a very old stereoscope and many glass slides. When I slide them into the stereoscope, I see my great-grandparents, my grand-aunt, and my grandfather in 3D, in their dress of the day, sitting at the dinner table enjoying a meal.

The oil paintings that now adorn my Tennessee home appear on the slides on the walls of my ancestors home at the end of the 19th century. I have quite a collection of his paintings, each one more magnificent than the other. My favorite is the one that features his next door neighbors in their typical costume of the region of Burgundy, or that of the old neighbors opening a letter.

Some of the slides date back to 1890. There is an old merry-go-around, and another carnival ride that looks like an instrument of torture. There are the ladies, dressed in their finest clothing, long gloves and immense hats, headed for church. Looking at them, I am literally transported one hundred years into the past.

I close my eyes and I see the home place, everyone working hard, laughing, eating and drinking. I smell the orchard, and the lavender sachets that always filled the drawers in great-grandmother's closets, and I picture great-grandfather carving a wooden shoe or putting the finishing touch on one of his paintings.

I try to return to Esnoms-au-Val as often as I can, but as I get older, it is becoming increasingly difficult to make the long, arduous trip. No matter. All I have to do is sit in my bedroom with a good cup of coffee, surrounded by my great-grandfather's paintings and touch the patina of the armoire.

Jean Nicholas Bourguignon would be astonished if he knew where the fruit of his labor ended-up one hundred years later. How I hope my two sons will take care of the legacy he left behind after I am gone.

FRANCINE FUQUA

Francine Fuqua is an author, an artist, and a lover of life. She is working on a sequel to her first novel, In Pursuit of Abraham. *She lives in Chattanooga, Tennessee. Connect with Francine at francinefuqua.com and read more about her French history and her vivid memories of growing up in World War II.*

MY TIN SEWING KIT

VICTORIA R. CHOATE

As a little girl growing up in Lebanon, Pennsylvania I seldom saw my paternal grandmother, Evelyn Bohac. I always loved when Nana came to visit. She was a short, petite woman about four feet ten inches and had short dark curly hair. She and my step-grandfather, Tony lived in a small mobile home in a trailer park in Reading, about thirty-two miles away. In today's standards that's not very far but in the early 1960s, it was quite a distance.

I have very few memories of Nana except that she smoked and always offered us a peppermint life saver when she came. My father was an only child, so my three brothers and I were her only grandchildren. I don't ever remember receiving a birthday or Christmas gift from her. She may have sent a card, but never a tangible gift like a stuffed animal, doll or toy. Regardless, I loved her dearly.

During one visit Nana and Tony took us to see the Pagoda in Reading which was up a steep hill. They drove an old car with a strap behind the front seat. The three of us hung on for dear life as we drove up the curvy road. Another special occasion was one summer when I spent a few days with her and Tony in Reading. It was a treat to go downtown and see the trolley cars and big department stores. Their little mobile home was pink and we went to the central laundromat in the trailer court to do the laundry. I thought it was fascinating.

Nana had a fear of dentists and despite decayed teeth she refused to go for treatment. She would put wax on her teeth and an aspirin directly on the tooth that hurt. She was eventually diagnosed with mouth cancer and suffered tremendously. She was hospitalized for several months and had nickel- and dime-sized holes in her face where the flesh had wasted away from the cancer. She lost her sight and her ability to speak. Doctors shaved her beautiful curly hair at the back of her head and cut a nerve to alleviate the pain. I remember visiting her in the hospital and will never forget the horrible odor of decaying flesh and seeing her frail body lying unresponsive in the bed.

The doctors planned to cut the nerve on the other side of her head because she still had excruciating pain, but she died on September 28, 1962. I was eight years old, and I was heartbroken.

Her life ended so prematurely at the age of fifty-three. I cry when I consider how different our childhood might have been if we had been granted more time with Nana, but God knows best and sees the big picture. At least she was no longer in pain.

Not long after her death Tony came by our house with a small white paper bag with a few items that were Nana's. There was a small rectangular white clutch purse and a few pieces of jewelry. I've always treasured these items.

Then at some point later, Tony gave me a little oval Christmas tin that belonged to Nana, and it quickly became a very special keepsake—a reminder of my grandmother.

The festive red holiday tin eventually became my sewing kit. It is the perfect size and shape and has two metal handles which makes it easy to carry. It measures nine inches long by seven inches wide by two inches high. The original information with the contents is still clearly marked on the center of the lid, "Satin Finish Madison Mixed Hard Candies made by Brandle and Smith, Div. of Luden's Inc. Reading, PA." I searched the internet and learned it was made in the 1930s to 1940s.

It's whimsical. Christmas trees, holly, bells, candles, wreaths, carolers, and mistletoe decorate the tin's surfaces. An African-American man in top hat and tails carries a present.

During the summer months when I was about nine years old, I walked across town to Ann Kleinfelter's house. She was a family friend who taught me how to hand sew simple doll clothes, especially for my Barbie doll. My little sewing kit had all the necessities: a pair of scissors, needles straight pins and pin cushion, thread, and a 6 inch ruler. I felt so grown up as I walked alone to see Mrs. Kleinfelter. I was safe and on a mission. Completing each garment was a big accomplishment, and I thought they were wonderful.

In the 1960s, there was an annual event to collect used toys before Christmas, clean them up, fix them up, and then give the toys to the less fortunate children in the neighborhood. Every year I collected my outgrown toys and made my donations. I parted with all my dolls and toys, except my Barbie doll and her box of clothing that I had made, and many pieces that my Mother had made, as well.

I clung to my little tin sewing kit which I used until I started high school. It was replaced by a bigger clear plastic sewing box for Home Economics Class. My little oval sewing tin was put away in the attic until I married at eighteen. I've kept it in my cedar hope chest for the past forty years, and today, it safely holds three silk corsages inside. Hopefully one day, I can pass my little tin sewing kit on to a granddaughter or niece who will appreciate its special meaning.

Why have I kept this tin all these years? It brings back childhood memories of long, summer days when I learned to sew, when a child could walk across town without fear of abduction, when handmade toys were a display of self reliance and resourcefulness and when simple inexpensive and even used things were a sign of thrift and frugality. But more importantly, it's a reminder of Nana. I have felt her watching over me many times. Our time together was very short in this life, but I believe in eternal families, and one day, I will see her again.

Victoria R. Choate is a Senior Forecasting Analyst for a major flooring company in Northwest Georgia. She is an avid genealogist and family historian. In her spare time she enjoys reading, and one day, hopes to write a series of children's stories based on her husband's childhood.

GRANDMA'S BANDS OF GOLD

CHRISTINE ALEXANDER JENNISON

"He's giving me the rings!" I said to myself.

I had just walked in the door at Grandma and Grandpa Charlie's house, ready to take Grandpa Charlie to his doctor's appointment. "Wait just a minute, I have something to give you" he mumbled as he walked into his bedroom. "Grandma wants you to have these." Grandpa acted like he had just had a conversation with Grandma, but she had passed away three years before.

In the early 1970s, my grandmother was diagnosed with, and lost her right leg to diabetes. She had several lifestyle changes due to the disease, one of them being to be more careful with her hands and feet. I don't really remember how I became her manicurist, but I did. Each time she visited my parent's house, I would manicure her hands.

In the thirty-five years since she passed away, sadly I cannot recall the features of her face, but I remember her hands. Grandma Bowman had beautiful hands. Her fingers were long and lean. Her Portuguese skin was a warm shade of brown. Her nails were strong yet pretty, not like mine that I bit down to the quick. She didn't make a big fuss over her nails. I don't ever remember putting a colored polish on her finger nails, but I always commented on how pretty her hands were, and how beautiful her wedding rings were. "You can have these rings when I die, Dolly," she always reminded me when I commented on the beauty of her rings. "When she dies?" I thought to myself. She's never going to die. I couldn't imagine a world without my grandmother.

I'm not exactly sure when my grandmother and Grandpa Charlie met, but they were married at the end of World War II, in California in 1945. Grandpa Charlie was already divorced, and his children lived in upstate New York. My grandmother divorced her first husband—my Grandpa Alexander—and left her four sons in California to move to Upstate New York with the man she loved.

Now, if you were to tell me this story, and my grandmother was not the main character, I would not think well of a woman who leaves her children behind to be with the man she loved. But, my grandmother was a loving and persuasive woman. After several years, she convinced my grandfather in California, to allow the two youngest boys to live with her and Grandpa Charlie. One of those boys who came from California was my father, and Grandpa Charlie became his father.

After Grandma died, I waited patiently for Grandpa to give me her wedding rings. Her wedding band was gold with one sparkling diamond in the middle, and her engagement ring had a large diamond in the middle with two smaller diamonds on each side. These pieces of jewelry always seemed somewhat magical to me, and I anticipated wearing them. But, after waiting for three years, I thought that perhaps Grandpa forgot. How could I tactfully bring up the rings? After all, these were the rings he had given to a woman that he loved and cherished, a woman who wore the rings until he tenderly removed them from her lifeless fingers. As he did so, perhaps he heard "until death do us part" in the back of his mind, but I know he meant forever. He would love her and be married to her *forever*.

So on this ordinary day, Grandpa decided to give the rings to *me*. I couldn't speak. I couldn't even say thank you at first when I accepted them. All I could do was give him a big hug and hold him tightly for a long while.

I slipped the rings on for the first time for a blind date. I wore them on my right hand. After that, I only wore the rings on special occasions.

Four months later, Barry-the-blind-date asked me to marry him, and I said, "Yes."

"Let's go to the jewelers and pick out our rings." Barry said that night. "What kind of rings do you like?"

"Well, I have my grandma's wedding rings, and they are very special to me," I replied. "We could have one of her diamonds reset."

We married in 1981. A few years later, I had the larger diamond from the middle of the wedding ring reset and my keepsake became my wedding ring from Barry. I stored the remains of the rings in my jewelry box, where I took them out and visited them from time to time, always remembering my grandmother and Grandpa Charlie.

In 2006, my niece, Alivia Dorothy Alexander was born. My brother and his wife gave Alivia my grandmother's name, Dorothy, for her middle name. I racked my brain trying to come up with a Christening present for Alivia. I wanted it to be special, something meaningful, not a ceramic angel, or baptism book, or something superfluous. I wanted my gift to be something sacred.

It was a week before the Christening and I still had no idea what to give to Alivia. I walked past my stand up jewelry box and thought of my grandmother's rings. I hadn't looked at the rings or thought about them for a long time. That's when I had an epiphany; I will take the band with the diamond in the middle to the jeweler and have him make the ring into a cross.

"I know this is short notice, but could you make this ring into a cross and keep the diamond in the middle?" I pleaded with the jeweler.

He studied the band with his eyepiece and then looked at me.

"And could you have it ready in a week?" I added.

He granted my wish as if he was the jewelry genie. I purchased a beautiful gold chain on which to hang the cross, and Alivia Dorothy wore it for her Christening.

And then, that day at the church, it came to me, as if my grandmother was telling me herself—Alivia could wear the cross not only for her Christening but also for her first communion, confirmation, and when she becomes a *bride*.

Grandma's wedding rings had come full circle, blessing more than just me with her bands of gold. And today, they remain symbols of timeless, endless love.

Christine Alexander Jennison enjoys the study of family ancestry, and travel, which has included an ancestral visit to the Azore Islands. She has traveled to several different states and European countries and has lived in Rabat, Morocco with her Air Force husband. Chris has been an avid volunteer most of her life, including Girl Scouts, Officer's Wives Club activities, and opportunities through her church. She is currently attending Chattanooga State Community College part-time and enjoys scrapbooking and documenting her family history. She is thankful to her neighbor Janie, for encouraging her to write.

THE FARM TABLE

MARVIN LEWIS

The oldest member of our family arrived in December of 2011. The simple draw-leaf farm table was crafted from a cherry tree that witnessed the French Revolution, perhaps by an aging revolutionary. It easily serves twelve—more when women and children are included. The worms that inscribed the leaves over the years possessed an art form belonging only to them.

It's history intrigues me. I often wonder what this table has witnessed. The political unrest and frequent change of the 1800s, an artistic revolution, and a cholera epidemic were certainly part of its history. But what else? I wonder what persons—famous or not—may have shared a meal or a bottle of wine over its surface.

Within the family, what transpired over nearly two hundred years? Over the five, six, or seven generations? Was there a mother who died in childbirth? A young bride who inherited a family older than she? It's experienced the birth and death of generation after generation. What kind of lives did they lead? Simple? Heroic? Did the families struggle to survive or enjoy prosperity?

How many people shared a feast or just managed to survive while discussing their hopes and dreams, sorrows and tribulations around this table?

Our table witnessed two world wars. Were family members wounded or killed? Did occupying troops feast at this table? Or perhaps it was the liberators—our brave, scared, tired, heroic, frightened young Americans. Was a Jewish family shielded from the concentration camps and near-certain death? Or, was the patriarch a German collaborator?

The post-war years were difficult. The elation of VE day in 1945 gave way to the reality of rebuilding a country devastated by war. As the modern era evolved, perhaps the table was cast aside in favor of chrome and Formica—something easier to care for—ushering in an end to the past and a focus on the New Age.

Perhaps our table was condemned to an outbuilding, not knowing its fate after years of faithfully serving the family.

Our table holds many secrets within its elegant wood grain. If only it could talk, it would certainly reveal a unique history all its own. Perhaps it's nothing exotic, just a simple life.

Thankfully, whatever its fate of recent years, a seasoned antique dealer rescued the table on his 99th trip to France, and then, we purchased it and vowed to give it the prominence and respect it so richly deserves.

For years to come, we plan to enjoy family, friends, and our many animals gathered around this table, feeling lucky to be a part of its history.

MARVIN LEWIS

Marvin Lewis is a graduate of Georgia Tech with BS and MS degrees in Textiles. Retired after thirty-seven years associated with the carpet industry, Marvin currently works in plastics recycling. His interests include sports, the arts, travel, community service, animal rescue and architecture. Marvin designed and supervised construction of two additions to the 1936 home he shares with his wife of thirty-two years, Joanne.

THE OLD CRANK TELEPHONE

PHYLLIS QUALLS FREEMAN

Bbrriinnggg. Bbrriinnggg.

Our son, Kent, turned the crank a couple of times before he and Daris secured the phone to a section of wall between their great room and the open kitchen.

We'd moved into a two-room suite in our son's new home. Not having room for everything from our house, we downsized to the benefit of the church yard sale. We couldn't part with some objects. The oak telephone from the early 1900s was one piece we'd kept. We hoped our children would hold that treasure tightly in their hearts and keep it, sharing its story.

In 1964, our red Corvair headed toward the tiny town of Herman, Minnesota. Nineteen hours of driving with two small children was a challenge, but we'd done it before. My husband

Bill's mom lived there and we planned to see her and other members of the extended family.

One of the side trips we took while visiting in Herman was north three hours to the city of Bemidji.

As we paid the admission to the Paul Bunyan Center, our two and four year olds ran ahead. They entered the Center and heard the overhead speaker; "Welcome, Kimberly and Kent Freeman from Cincinnati, Ohio."

The children peered guardedly around to see who knew them. The clerk at the gate had inquired about their names.

The folklore lumberjack hero Paul Bunyan and his blue ox Babe were impressive statues and made the stories larger than life.

We took another side trip while in Minnesota, to see Bill's Uncle Harvey Richards. Mom Freeman arranged for us to visit their home set among numerous green pine trees.

I didn't realize that sweaty-child predators—*ticks*—lurked in the trees and in the grass where the children played that day. *Yikes!* In Cincinnati, we didn't live near woods and were unaware of the dangers. Aunt Margie warned me to check over the kids, and much to my dismay, I picked several bloated black ticks off the children on the way home. That evening, I put the children in a warm, sudsy tub after doing a strip-search on each of them.

While I fought the battle of ticks, Uncle Harvey showed Bill his collection of antique phones. Uncle Harvey opened up the body of each phone, placed a radio inside, and sold the unit as a phone-radio. He offered to do this for my husband, but Bill wanted the phone in its original condition. My husband selected an early 1900s' model and carried it to the car with pride. The beautiful oak piece held a prominent place in our small home. Now, almost fifty years later, we still have the lovely chunk of history.

THE OLD CRANK TELEPHONE

Through the years, so many of our friends lifted the ear piece (with the old cord still attached), rang the bell, and pretended to talk to the operator.

Why would someone want to keep an outdated, non-working piece of wood? *Memories.*

I have a few memories of my Grandmother Qualls using a similar antique crank phone. *Bbrriinnggg, bbrriinnggg.* Yes, you rang the bell to talk to the operator.

"Hello, Myrtle, please ring Ola Duncan."

"Oh, hello Miss Minnie. Everyone at your house okay?" the operator would ask.

"Fine, Myrtle. Just get Ola, please."

Granddaddy Qualls was issued a telephone, similar to the one we obtained, by the fire fighter's service in the 1930s, when he was the warden of forest fires for Perry County, Tennessee. Granddaddy's phone's *ring* was two short rings and a long one. He had a crew of eight to ten neighbor men who were on his team.

When the lookout man in the tower rang the Qualls' farmhouse to say there was a nearby blaze, Aunt Mona rode the mule to notify some of the men while Granddaddy roused others to help fight the fire. The men walked miles carrying their fire-rakes to the burning field or farm. They used heavy-handled rakes to clean out small brush and bushes to keep the fire from spreading. Sometimes they stayed at the site of the fire for days. When the blazes and smoke were safely extinguished, the men walked miles back to their own farms to resume their own work.

Today, Bill and I have moved into the 21st century with our own cell phones, but we still like to hear the *bbrriinnggg* from the old one occasionally. It always elicits a smile.

Since we relocated to Hixson, Tennessee, our new friends and those of Kent and Daris sometimes crank the phone just to listen to the bell's buzzy ring. It's a friendly ring with memories attached, and I hope it will bring a smile as it rings on for another century.

Phyllis Qualls Freeman is a writer and speaker who lives in Hixson, Tennessee with her husband, Bill. She crafts devotionals, human interest, and newspaper articles. She also writes Life Related Learnings *for Pathway Press, and devotionals for Reflections, Smyth & Hewlys and for Standard Publishing's Devotions. Phyllis teaches classes and workshops on emotional healing issues, and other topics. She is working on a book of stories about those who have moved through traumatic life experiences and come to a place of peace.*

MATTIE BELL'S BIBLE

MISSIONARY JANIE AKER

In the spring of 1987, my father's sister, Mattie Bell Goudlock Lattimore died. She shared a small farmhouse in Dahlonega, Georgia with her husband of thirty-six years, who died five years before her. As a child, my family would celebrate the holidays at Aunt Mattie Bell and Uncle Moses' house. And when I was a teenager, my girlfriend, Margaret and I would often board a bus and travel the seventy-mile winding road to Aunt Mattie Bell's house for a weekend—just to get away from home for a little while.

Aunt Mattie Bell was a kind and peaceful woman who drew the admiration of her family, friends, and community. She had a strong work ethic—maintaining a job as a housekeeper for a family in Dahlonega for several years. And she loved to cook, or maybe she just liked being by herself in the kitchen. Either way, Aunt Mattie Bell's cooking was heavenly, and everyone looked forward to tasting and devouring her meals and desserts.

So understandably, I was heartbroken when she died. She and Uncle Moses didn't have any children, and their hard-earned possessions were divided among family members and friends shortly after her passing. I still remember walking through the emptying house full of memories, and that's when I saw it—Aunt Mattie Bell's family Bible.

I immediately felt a strong connection with her Bible and picked it up. I didn't know that she was a spiritual person, but apparently she was, because the Bible was worn with love—the brown leather cover was scarred and the pages showed evidence that they had been read and re-read and re-read. Joy filled my heart, and I knew that I wanted Aunt Mattie Bell's Bible. It was the only memento that I took home that day.

The old Bible is not only a priceless reminder of my beloved aunt, it is also a representation of my faith. You see, there was a time in my life when I felt lost spiritually. We had Bibles around our house but I didn't read them very often. The scripture was hard for me to understand, so our Bibles mostly sat on tables and collected dust.

But deep inside, I had a burning desire to know Jesus and feel his love. I never felt smart in school or in life in general, and so I never truly believed that God noticed me. I never thought that He could *use* me in any way. But that changed one glorious day when I was listening to a local radio broadcast. The preacher on the radio told the story of David. I stopped and considered the story.

David, once a commoner, led an imperfect life and did many bad things, and yet, God said that David was a man after his own heart. David repented his sins and gained God's favor. He rose to power and eventually became King of Israel.

I began reading the Psalms. They were like poetry to me and I began to understand them. I prayed for more knowledge and wisdom, and like David, I, too, repented my sins and asked for a personal relationship with Jesus Christ. *And I received it!*

One Sunday as I sang in the church choir, I felt a supernatural presence beside me. I felt my lord touch me on my shoulder and a fiery sensation like electricity moved through me from my fingers to my toes. It's hard to explain, but His touch brought me elation, brought me calm, brought me new life, and I was never the same again.

After that day, I looked at the Bible in a completely different light—it's not just a book, it is my personal road map to salvation. Everything I need to know to see my savior one day is written there in black and white. I realized the Holy word will lead me to God. And I finally understood that if I have the word inside of me, that no one can ever take that wisdom away. If my golden years take my sight from me and I can no longer read my Bible, I'll still have the Word in my heart forever.

And God began to *use* me. He gave me a grand purpose and I began preaching at a small church in Calhoun, Georgia and performing mission work for my community—clothing people who need clothing, visiting with the sick, helping with funerals, and other duties that God assigns to me.

But I start each day by opening Aunt Mattie Bell's Bible and reading and thinking and praying with my husband of fifty-three years, Preston Aker, Sr. It's somewhat ironic that the Bible that I acquired after my aunt's death has given me life—a life that I never imagined

In 1981, God helped Janie Aker and her husband, Preston, open a church mission—the Mission of All God's Children—in

MISSIONARY JANIE AKER

Calhoun, Georgia, where they spread His word, feed the hungry, clothe the poor, and help the disadvantaged get health and medical services. The couple has three grown children—Preston, Matasha, and Rodney.

MEMENTOS OF A FREEMASON

KEN BERRY

Attempting to restrain tears, my grief-stricken mother entered my bedroom early on a dreary February morning and sat at the side of my bed. She told me my father had died during the night. I sat up trying to grasp what she was saying as she reached out to hand me his Masonic ring. Tradition called for this ring to be passed down to the oldest male in the family, she added blankly, like the swords and shields of medieval knights killed in battle were bequeathed to first-born sons.

I was fifteen. I knew nothing of medieval knights. My father's small electrical business in our farming community in Western Montana was just starting to prosper. I can still see him beaming with pride from the cab of a *new* used truck he had recently purchased. Hospitalized after suffering a heart attack two days earlier, he was alert and in good spirits the previous evening when I last visited with him.

I glanced at the simple gold band, adorned only with a single letter of the Hebrew alphabet enclosed in an equilateral triangle. The ring was too large to fit any of my fingers but there would be plenty of time to grow into it, my mother noted, since the requisite age to become a Freemason is twenty-one.

Attaining the three degrees of a Master Mason a decade earlier, my father eventually attained the lofty post of Worshipful Master, a lodge's presiding officer. Along the way he had also joined an associate organization offering twenty-nine additional Masonic degrees, completing fifteen of them before his death. The ring had been presented to him following the conferral of the 14th degree, a milestone in the Ancient and Accepted Scottish Rite of Freemasonry.

My father had worked himself to death and our family was left penniless. Along with my two younger siblings, my mother and I packed our belonging and moved away to seek opportunities offered in a bigger city, eventually losing track of friends and even my father's relatives. During the several years of upheaval that followed, I somehow managed *not* to lose track of my father's ring.

Years later, my best friend, Charlie, helped strap the oxygen tank to my back as I prepared to make my maiden scuba dive. I was in my early twenties. Montana's Flathead Lake, the third largest body of fresh water in the nation and a haven for boaters in the summer remains cold all year long. Earlier, as I had donned a wetsuit my three companions gave me a pep talk and a safety check of sorts. We were not certified divers; we were college kids. Only Charlie had previously ventured underwater with diving gear—on a single occasion.

Beneath ominous gray clouds that were spewing intermittent rain, the dark green tide slapped against the rocky shore. Whitecaps in the distance explained the absence of pleasure craft. Fearful of water since childhood, my feelings about this particular adventure were mixed. I was already shivering, with no gloves or booties to keep my hands and feet warm. I wore my father's ring on my left hand while an identical gold band that had been presented to me upon becoming a 14th degree Mason the previous year was tucked away in a shoebox at my mother's house, perhaps to someday be passed on to a son of my own.

As my partner finished suiting up, I stumbled clumsily into the water, breathing from my tank and ignoring the agony inflicted by the floor of jagged stones upon my bare feet. After several steps the water reached my chest and I lunged forward, slipping below the surface.

Charlie had emerged from the depths only thirty minutes earlier along with his dive partner, an expert swimmer he met during high school. The son of a county sheriff, Charlie had persuaded his former classmate to join our expedition after finagling two sets of diving gear from his dad's search and rescue department.

Equipped with the same gear Charlie had used, I swam away from the shore along the murky bottom. I could see through my leaky mask boulders the size of watermelons and occasional sea cucumbers that were half buried in silt. Adrenaline raced through my body as I eventually slowed, apprehensive about the water accumulating in my mask as well as my sudden inability to breathe easily. Glancing up and around me, I was unable to see my partner. Then oxygen stopped flowing from my tank.

Sheer panic gripped me as I struggled for air, flailing wildly toward the surface. The seconds seemed like minutes before I burst through the surface, gasping and ripping the breathing apparatus from my mouth. After struggling some seventy-five yards back to shore under the additional weight of my gear, I was handed a beer and the joking that would continue for years began: Would a true friend give another an empty tank for a dive? Aren't empty tanks usually reserved for airheads? It could have been worse because twin tanks are heavier.

The four of us stood around a warm fire laughing before I realized my father's 14th degree ring had slipped from my hand during the ordeal, and that its recovery from the muddy bottom of the lake would be impossible.

My despair upon opening my shoebox the following day to retrieve my identical ring was overwhelming. I no longer possessed anything belonging to my father. For a moment I admired the glimmering band that had been presented to me by Scottish Rite Masons in Missoula, pondering the appropriate direction of the triangle's apex before sliding it onto my finger. I had not returned to a Masonic lodge following my initiation, nor did I view my own ring then as I would in coming years: a valued keepsake reminding me of my father's most precious gift.

Like the unique order of crusading knights whose history they embrace, Freemasons value character and civility. Lessons gleaned from the Knights Templar and their last grand master, Jacques DeMolay—who in 1314 was slow-burned at the stake in Paris for his refusal to utter falsehoods in order to save himself—are central to many of their degrees.

"In Masonry, it's not the degrees that matter most," said one Masonic official. "It's how you treat your fellows, and how you behave in your communities."

The goal of modern day Masonry is to make good men better.

"Strive not to be better than others," leaders admonish, "but to be better than yourself."

Some men become Masons seeking fraternity. Others fascinated with allegories and symbolism seek enlightenment about Masonic influence on the world or American history. Seventeen U.S. presidents have become Masons. Some join to give back—Freemasons in the United States donate nearly $2 million each day to charitable causes.

Scottish Rite brands itself as "a network of men you can trust." During biennial sessions in the nation's capital, Scottish Rite recognizes exemplary service by conferring an honorary 33rd degree on selected longtime members. More than twenty-five years after my initiation, while living in Hawaii, I became an honored recipient. Had he been looking down on the proceedings, my father would have been proud. I was also presented with the official ring of the degree, and my keepsake ring—worn since my Flathead Lake misadventure—was returned to my shoebox.

In 2007, Easter activities at the First Christ Church in Yankton, South Dakota, mesmerized my Hawaiian-born wife of Japanese ancestry. Raised Buddhist she was in her forties as she gleaned a life-changing taste of Christianity, savoring the pomp and splendor of Episcopal revelry as well as the Yankton parish's warm hospitality.

While living in Hawaii, a chance meeting with a tourist in Waikiki led us to discover my father's favorite sister was alive and well some forty-five years after his death. On a Good Friday, we showed up on her doorstep in Yankton, a city of 80,000 in the southeastern corner of the state, just across the Missouri River from Nebraska. My aunt and uncle, a Freemason who had once served as mayor of Yankton, drove us to countless area landmarks and scenic lookouts, insisting that we join them for meals and accompany them to festivities at their beloved church.

Established in 1861, the "Mother Church of the Dakotas" showcases woodwork, rood screens, alter hangings and kneelers that reflect the resourcefulness and artistic talent of its devoted parishioners. The only first-time visitors at Sunday's Easter service, my wife and I were introduced to the large congregation. People who live in Yankton must love Yankton, we concluded when a member greeted me following the service. "I remember your father," he said pointing to the third pew. "He used to sit right there."

Following dinner at her home that evening my aunt slipped away from the dining table and returned with a box of mementos. Smiling, she gave me several photographs of my father that I had never seen—as a youth pictured with his basketball and baseball teams and in uniform after his enlistment in the U.S. Navy. Handing me a handsome medallion my father had won eighty years earlier at a regional high school track meet, my aunt said it was a keepsake that she wanted me to have. Made of sterling silver with a bronze inset, an inscription on the back revealed it had been awarded for winning first place in a sprint.

"Now this really is a keepsake," I thought to myself as I thanked her, vowing to shine it up and wear it around my neck, forever.

Alone on a sunny morning later that year, I climbed a mountain ridge in Kahana Valley on the Hawaiian island of Oahu. To the uninitiated, running toward the edge of a cliff and flinging yourself into the air can seem suicidal. To those devoted to the extreme sport of paragliding, only two terrible things can happen in the life of an enthusiast: hucking yourself into the air *knowing* it will be your last huck, or hucking yourself into the air *not knowing* it will be your last huck.

I launched into gentle, easterly winds sweeping over a picturesque bay below. Strapped into my harness connected by an array of thin lines to the nylon canopy above, tradewinds would provide updrafts sufficient to float above the panoramas below.

Within an hour, other "pilots" followed a trail to favored launch sites. Five were already in the air as I began my descent toward a distant beach, enjoying breathtaking views of giant sea turtles in the distance and fishermen tending to their lines from a nearby pier below. My landing in the soft, white sand of the empty beach was flawless and I allowed my canopy to float above me momentarily so that airborne pilots might note the prevailing wind direction on shore.

With my back to the ocean I faced a deep pond interrupting a strip of tall pines separating the beach from an adjacent highway. Collapsing my canopy, the wing fell softly to the sand before I released the controls from my hands to unbuckle my leg straps. Then, everything went very bad. Without warning, a rogue gust violently yanked my canopy into the air, instantly thrusting it with me helplessly in tow, over the sand and into the pond. I grasped in vain for control lines that would dampen the wing as I was pulled off my feet and head first into the water. Then as suddenly as I was jerked from my feet and flung through the air, I was deposited in the midst of the 10-foot-deep pond where it was still.

For a fleeting moment, I found the irony amusing. Despite a perfect launch, smooth flight and flawless landing I would need to clean my canopy of sand and salt water, and likely replace my radio and altimeter that were now submerged. Treading water, alarm replaced amusement when I was unable to unhook my leg straps to free myself from my harness. Too, I was alone. I had seen no one on the beach, a moot point since the pines hide the pond from the view of most picnickers and swimmers, and a high bridge above the pond conceals it from traversing vehicles.

Terror replaced alarm as I attempted to swim the few feet to safety only to find my legs entangled in canopy lines that restricted their movement. At the same time, I discovered I was hopelessly anchored by my gear to the pond's bottom, preventing my movement toward safety. Though my harness was buoyant, only treading actively with both arms would keep my head above water and prevent me from rolling to either side. The frantic life and death struggle that ensued lasted an eternity for me, but only about twenty-five minutes in real time.

Unable to breathe without treading I became exhausted, repeatedly swallowing brackish water while sinking beneath the surface in frantic attempts to free myself. In a final moment of consciousness, it seemed clear that I would die. Incredibly, as I began to accept my fate a second gust swept up a wingtip, the only dry section of my twenty-five-foot wing remaining atop the water's surface, thrusting it a few feet toward a concrete pillar supporting the bridge above me. Like an action film in which the hero avoids certain death due to some implausible event, my wingtip leapt forward, then upward to snag on a small nail. I scoff at such scenes in movies but will always see the inexplicable movement of my wingtip out of the pond as a miracle. Suddenly I was able to lie still in my harness with my face out of the water. I passed out with no one near me.

Eerie tales of spirits and supernatural encounters emanate regularly from Kahana Valley. Following her only hike with me to a nearby launch site, my wife claimed she experienced an extraordinary dread beneath the jungle canopy under which she passed alone on her downhill trek.

"If one can figure out when the night of no moon falls," writes a popular Hawaii author about legendary spirits setting forth from area jungles to reclaim ancient land lost to Westerners, "then he or she will have the fortune or misfortune of being there when they make their way to the Bay. One should be prepared for an unforgettable encounter that will change a life."

The incredible combination of factors that placed me in a near-death situation was unfathomable: The rare gust. The tiny but deep pond created by infrequent seasonal weather aberrations. A passerby who disappeared after refusing to step a few inches into the water with a tree limb—because he could not swim. A nearby fire station dismissing a report of my distress after radioing a leader of our airborne fraternity who responded the alarm was unjustified; he was at the scene and, with the exception of one pilot who had landed safely earlier, all who had launched remained in the air with him.

Coming to on the beach where I had landed earlier, my rescuers helped remove my gear. Unzipping the upper part of my flight suit I noticed that my father's medallion had been ripped from my neck during the ordeal; I had begun wearing it only days earlier. Finding it moments later with a broken clasp, trapped in a pant leg that remained tucked in my boot, I stuffed it in a pocket of the surf shorts I wore underneath my flight suit.

Following my hapless dive at Flathead Lake, an art student fascinated with the metaphysical and unimpressed with fraternity boys like Charlie and me opined that my father may have wanted his ring back due to my indifference to Masonic principles. It was not lost on me that my only possessions of his had been wrested from my body as I struggled to avoid watery fates.

Lying near the pond, exhausted and surrounded by a crowd attracted by flashing lights or sirens, I mouthed a silent prayer of gratitude, sensing that a higher power indeed had reached out to rescue me from whatever forces I had grappled with.

Freemasonry is not a religious organization though members profess a belief in a higher power, a supreme architect. The Bible and Koran are among sacred books placed upon altars to illustrate Masonic devotion to religious freedoms. Invariably during reverent interludes in the Honolulu auditorium where Scottish Rite Masons assemble, I find myself gazing toward a high outcropping where a large triangle within a circle commemorates the 14th degree and a Mason's quest for knowledge.

Sometimes I say a silent prayer for my father. Sometimes I close my eyes to see his new used truck pulling into our driveway. I see him standing beneath a large oak tree lobbing a baseball to my younger brother and me, and then catching our errant throws. I see him at our small kitchen table enjoying the meager meal prepared by my mother following her workday at our store.

Sometimes I see his large hands, scratched from daily tussles with wires and junction boxes, stained with soap-resistant grime. As my mother and father debate the viability of Adlai Stevenson's new running mate in the forthcoming presidential election, I see on his ring finger the gold band with the triangle enclosing the Hebrew character Yod that lies buried in mud and debris beneath Flathead Lake.

In 2012, after many years of Freemasonry, I was named to a high position that few before me have held. My father would be extremely proud of the appointment. He would be pleased that I became increasingly active in his beloved fraternity as well as a better, more compassionate person.

Like his track medallion with the broken clasp, my own 14th degree ring representing his ultimate gift to me, presented by long-forgotten Freemasons in Montana, will not be worn again. On rare occasions when I hold in my hands the two keepsakes evoking vivid remembrances of my father and his personage, I'm overcome with emotion. They are never too far out of mind though they remain out of sight, tucked away in a shoebox in a closet at my home in Hawaii.

After living in Chattanooga, Tennessee for a few years, Ken Berry moved back to Hawaii where he and his wife, Karen, own a media consultant company. In his spare time, he enjoys sailing through the skies above the islands in his paraglider.

THE OLD IRON BED

MARTHA BUTTRUM

The keepsake I cherish most, is an old iron bed frame. I bought it twenty-six years ago from a second hand store. I have no idea how old it is or who previously owned it. I sanded it, painted it white, touched-up the artwork on the center panels of its headboard and footboard, and replaced the old fashioned wire springs and cotton mattress with box springs and a pillow top mattress. In fact, the box springs and mattress sets have been replaced about three times in the past twenty-six years.

The bed has been passed around in my family with the understanding that it stays in *my* family. It is currently being used by my youngest son's in-laws.

No one I have ever known spent their first married night in that bed. No one I have ever known was born in that bed. No one I have ever known died in that bed. To anyone and everyone else, the bed is just an old iron bed frame—something to take up space in a room—just a simple place to rest for awhile. But to me, it is much more than just a bed. It is more precious to me than diamonds or gold.

On Labor Day in 1983, Mama, Daddy, my kids (Daisy, Lamar, Leigh, Jake, Eric) and I attended a barbecue lunch at the local VFW. Afterwards we strolled in downtown Calhoun, just enjoying the holiday and the end of summer. Mama noticed an antique sewing machine on display in the window of a store, prompting us to go in and browse. The shop was full of wonderful, discarded treasures marked down to bargain prices. A ceramic dog missing a tail and an ear for $1.50, a rusty water bucket with a rustier dipper for $3.50, a Shirley Temple doll missing an eye for $5.00 (Shirley was still quite popular regardless of the deformities), but it was a brown, rust-laden iron bed frame that got my attention, and it was only $65. So I made a lay-a-way deal with $10 down and $10 every Friday with a final payment of $15 to be paid in early October.

The payment plan was working out just fine until one Friday when I worked late and the store closed before I could get by. I was scheduled to work the following day as well, so I gave the $10 payment to Daddy. I also gave him an extra $20 for his trouble or to take my kids out to eat, do something fun—*fun money*, we called it—or whatever.

The following Friday, when I ran by the store after work to make my payment, the gentleman behind the counter said, "Honey, you only owe $5 and you can take your bed on home with you."

I told him he was mistaken. I knew how much I had paid and how much I still owed. He just laughed and shook his head, "No, Ma'am, I'm not mistaken. It's right here on this card. Your daddy come in here last week and paid $30."

I thanked the gentleman and carried my bed home.

When I asked Daddy why he paid the whole $30 and why he didn't hold back the *fun money*, he said he knew how much I wanted that bed.

"The youngins' didn't go hungry," he said. "And we had fun without spending any extra money."

Daddy even helped me refinish the bed, and when we finished the project, it was beautiful. All he asked of me was that I let him "try it out," so he took a two hour nap on that bed one summer afternoon and was very pleased.

Daddy died the following year as he suffered from congestive heart failure, and that's when the old iron bed frame was transformed into my most prized possession—*a keepsake*. It had nothing to do with the bed frame itself. It had everything to do with a father's love for his daughter and how he would spend his last penny just to make her happy. Bed or no bed, I was always happy just being my daddy's daughter.

I've told this story many times using it as a personal testimony. If my earthly Father loved me *that* much, just imagine how much more my Heavenly Father loves me.

My children are all grown and they all know the story of the bed frame by heart, so now it's their turn to share the story with their children and grandchildren and so on, and so on. As I age, the story gets sweeter. I think that maybe someday when the bed makes it's way back to my house, I'll set it up in a special room and use it to display the handmade quilts Mama left behind as reminders of a mother's love. But that's another story . . .

Martha Buttrum is retired and lives in North Georgia near her five children and eight grandchildren. In her spare time she enjoys sewing, reading, writing poetry and short stories and playing with the grandchildren.

CIRCUS TEDDY BEAR

ELIZABETH SWAFFORD

Walking into the center ring of a three ring circus, a young, light grey elephant slowly swung its trunk back and forth as its handler led the way. Giddy children, and lively adults, sitting on the curved rim of the circus ring during the pre-show stared at the four-legged wonder, genuinely enthralled at seeing an elephant up close for the first time. Getting a look at an elephant or two at the zoo or on television was one thing, you could see them from a distance and know that they are simply huge impressive creatures. In person however, they were epic. The smallest member of the circus' elephant herd walked along the edge of the center ring making its way towards me and the little children sitting next to me.

Rotund plumpness stood just a foot from my face, so close I could hardly believe it was actually there. I could see every deep wrinkle, every wiry hair, and hear each of its heavy foot steps pound the concrete floor beneath us. The elephant tilted its head just a bit and looked me straight in the eye, as if it were greeting me. The colorful circus lights above formed a bright white gleam in its big round eyes fringed by the longest eyelashes ever to be part of such a young mammal.

"This little guy seems happy," I thought. *"Happy to be around the positive energy beaming from all the smiling faces watching him tonight."*

To everyone's delight the baby elephant, at least to me it was a baby still, began to paint. It skillfully held a large, gold paintbrush with its leathery trunk and carefully dipped it into a pot of bold, yellow paint. Waving its rough, curled trunk like a magician waves his wand, the baby touched paint to canvas and began to make a painting. It was amazing, almost like the creature recognized colors, shapes, and knew exactly what scene it intended to paint. A lot of strokes of green here, some red there, and a little bit of blue. By the end of the short painting session the canvas touched by the youngest elephant in the whole circus looked like a true piece of modern art. I had seen chimps paint on television before, but never an elephant, and never in person. I was just for a moment completely speechless. It was magic, of course.

As the music got louder an orange haired clown handed me an individually wrapped bright, red, plastic something from his giant, red bucket. While opening the small packet I laughed realizing it was a classic, round, red clown nose. I turned around and showed it to my husband who was seated on the bench behind me.

"Put it on!" he shouted almost immediately, answering my question before I even asked.

So I did for a bit, along with the kids who were now trying to learn a dance from the cluster of clowns. The shiny, red clown nose pinched and blocked my nose from smelling the unmistakable scents of buttered popcorn, fresh hay, and sweet cotton candy making their way thru the arena. Reluctantly I removed it and tucked the small nose in my purse along with my husband's, still in its noisy, clear wrapper.

Glittering acrobats arrived in their diamond encrusted costumes of silver, and royal blue. Some began to juggle white and red striped bowling pins, while others jumped and flipped in mid air without any special equipment. Each time they spun around they brought the smell of freshly popped buttered corn closer, and closer to the center ring. I breathed in deeply and made a mental note to buy popcorn once we got to our seats for the main show. Music played, people danced, an acrobat hoola hooped six rainbow colored hoops. Clowns in oversized shoes made pure joy bubble-up inside of everyone, bringing it out in audible giggles. It was magic, of course.

The pre-show ended all too soon, the staff and performers waved us away from the center ring, urging the crowd to find their seats. My husband and I walked precariously up a flight of very narrow, steep, grey concrete stairs in the arena. I had somehow convinced him to take me to the circus that day. After all, it was guaranteed to be the "greatest show on earth" and couldn't be missed. I walked up the steps first as he held his left hand up behind me in case I fell. His right hand grabbed on tightly to the cold, metal hand rail. We moved slowly, each step we took very cautious, and purposeful. He glanced behind us for a brief moment.

"Oh my god! We're way too high!" he bellowed in my ear.

"So this is what the nose bleed section is like!" I mumbled to myself, not sure if my husband had heard me with the loud music, and bustling crowd of people around us. I knew the tickets were a bit last minute, but still, I was surprised we had ended up almost at the ceiling of the arena. Thankfully, we made it to our stadium seats just as a feeling of dizziness started to fog my head. I sat down on the cold, hard plastic chair, scooting my bottom back into it until I was certain that my whole body was in, seated, and secure.

As I looked around, hundreds of people were looking for their seats as they navigated around several vendors eager to sell cotton candy, snow cones, and circus souvenirs. Cautious parents of younger children grasped their child's hand so tightly that the little ones seemed to loose circulation to their whole arm by the time they got to their seats. The vendors in particular didn't seem to care about the heights they were walking thru while carrying all of their merchandise on what appeared to be tall, thin, white branches.

I leaned over to my husband, seated to my left, and whispered, "Thank you sweetheart."

It had been ages since I had been to a proper circus, and I wanted to capture some of the magic again. Where else could you see delicate, dancing elephants, terrifying tigers, and proud, prancing white horses all in one place? Being there and witnessing the agility of the acrobats, and the cleverness of the clowns made me wonder. Were all the things I saw there a result of figments of the audience's imagination, optical illusions, or possibly real magic? As I gazed at the center ring from high above, inside our concrete perch, I simply chose to believe that what happened at the circus was in fact *true magic*.

The rings below were blanketed with lavender, and gold stage lights just moments before a large group of white horses galloped loudly through the red, velvet curtain making a grand entrance.

"Yay! It started!" I smiled, and reached over to squeeze my husband's hand. We'd survived the trek to the tippy top of the arena, just in time to watch the circus unfold. The prancing horses looked so little from my seat high above the crowd. They seemed like horses fit for a band of fairies rather than the full size slender, tall, and graceful human performers riding them. Moments later the clowns came, playing gags on each other with entertaining props including a giant boom box. Upbeat music was constant, the lights kept moving, changing colors—if I didn't focus just on the center ring I would start to feel dizzy within seconds. In between acts I'd touch my husband's knee, just to make sure he was there. It was rather disconcerting to be up so high, but I made an effort to enjoy the show.

Tame tigers leaped onto large stools, eating meat off a stick as they stood on their hind legs following the cues of the trainer's whip. How could such an amazing and dangerous tiger act like a domesticated house cat? It was magic, of course. There was no other possible explanation, especially when ten orange and black striped tigers were all doing the same actions in unison. A lion roared, but I didn't dare to turn my head to find it.

High above the circus ring, but not quite as high up as we were, a man in a sparkling blue top and silver tights began walking on thin air. A spotlight momentarily illuminated a tight rope, but without the direct beams of light it appeared that he was tip toeing high above the floor in the middle of the arena with no ropes, no nets, no harnesses—*nothing*.

I leaned over and asked my husband, "How do you like the show so far?"

He was gripping the arm rest of the chairs so tight his knuckles were already a pale yellow. "I like the show, but I think I'm getting vertigo. I don't like it up here." he replied with a shaky voice.

I patted his leg a couple of times and thought, *"Ah, the sacrifices one makes for loved ones."* I knew he was more uncomfortable than me, but I was so happy to be at the circus that I quickly forgot about our discomforts.

Blue and pink balls of cotton candy in clear plastic bags caught my eye. I eagerly waved at the keeper of the cotton candy tree, and bought a bag of half pink and half blue, fluffy spun sugar. Cotton candy is a must have at the circus and the county fair. When the bag was finally opened the scent of sweetened sugar rushed to my nose like a delicate perfume. By the time I had a large piece of cotton candy dissolving in my mouth the man walking in thin air was riding a unicycle. I gazed wide-eyed as another piece of a wispy pink cloud melted in my mouth. It was magic, of course.

Other performers participated during the show; a lady spun on a rope attached by her long hair, a martial artist lunged through a ring of swords, and a duo performed with trained house cats that actually went to their crate when told. Each performance had it's own unique moment of wonderment that added to the magical feel of the whole evening. The circus ended with big fan fare, the whole lot of elephants, horses, and performers making a final appearance during an elaborate musical score. I sighed. For me, it ended too quickly.

Eventually my dizzy husband and I made our way to one of the gift shops selling a variety of circus souvenirs, and even some popcorn. Plastic drinking cups with lids shaped like the head of a lion were popular, so were the picture books that performers could autograph. What caught my eye was an adorable tiny light brown teddy bear with a black, triangle shaped nose, and round, shiny, black eyes sitting near the register.

He had a full outfit on—perfectly tiny blue jeans, a red sweatshirt with pockets, and a yellow baseball cap with two openings for his miniature rounded ears. The cotton sweatshirt had a blue, round iron-on that said in white letters, "The Greatest Show On Earth." And, the ball cap placed sideways on his head had a big blue "R" for Ringling Brothers embroidered just above the brim.

I passed on the popcorn, though the smell of the salted butter was tempting, and quickly purchased the tiny bear.

My husband and I walked out of the arena holding hands, navigating past the bustling crowd still excited about the amazing circus performance. In the late afternoon sun the outside of the arena looked dreary and depressing, lacking all sort of color on its gray outer shell.

I squeezed my new, brightly colored teddy bear with my available hand, holding the soft, small treasure close to my chest.

"What are you gonna name him?" my husband asked once we had found our car.

"Circus Bear." I announced.

"Well that's a great name! He looks colorful enough, and he's got the logo."

I placed the tiny bear on the car's dashboard so we both could see him as we drove home.

"Told ya it was going to be the greatest show on earth! Says so on his sweater."

We both laughed, and recounted the circus performance on our way home while Circus Bear listened.

My teddy bear from the circus is one of my favorite keepsakes. Even today it reminds me of the astute animals we saw perform, the colorful lights, and stunning costumes. But most of all, it reminds me of my husband who was sweet enough to take me and endure the dizzying heights at the arena. When I see the soft bear sitting on my night stand, I always smile knowing it's full of magic, of course.

Elizabeth Swafford lives in a historic mill town nestled in the mountains of North West Georgia with her husband Doyal, and their tiny dog named Phoebe. Liz spends her creative time writing, painting, and reading all sorts of interesting books.

THE RUBBER STAMP

TIM EGENES

The item once belonged to my father. In his working career, it was his identity. It is a small tubular rubber stamp which he used to verify that he had personally inspected and released for use, the many airplane parts he reviewed while on the job. A unique style and individual number indicated which employee had given his approval.

He worked for Lockheed California Company for over thirty-five years. He worked in many different jobs during his tenure, some of which we, as his family, never knew about until years later. He had a high level security classification, which allowed him to work on many secret projects during the height of the Cold War.

In his many years in the employ of Lockheed, he worked

on many different types of aircraft. He worked on propeller-powered aircraft such as the P-38 pursuit fighter, known as the "Fork Tailed Devil" by the German ground troops during World War II. In later years he worked on the P-3 Orion, F-104 Starfighters, C-130 Hercules, and C-141 Starlifter, and eventually the C-5 Galaxy cargo transport planes. He also worked in the now famous "Skunk Works" on planes such as the U-2 Dragon Lady, the YF-12-A, and SR-71 Blackbird, which to this day still holds most records for speed and altitude by standard air-breathing aircraft.

During his job as Flight Test Inspector, the small rubber stamp was his assurance that the parts he had inspected were in compliance and ready for flight. I'm sure his stamp still appears on many planes in many countries, though most of them are probably now in museums.

When my father retired from Lockheed in the late 1970s, he was given a framed picture of himself standing in front of an S-3A Viking carrier based jet. On the matting surrounding his picture are the signatures and well wishes of many of his coworkers. Each person also included his personal rubber stamp impression as a signature, which was their work-related identity.

When my father passed away, my siblings and I all gathered at my father's house and went through a lifetime of his possessions. Each of us chose to keep items that brought back memories only to that person. My brother found the small single-shot .22 caliber rifle he shot when he was a small boy with Dad's guidance. One of my sisters chose a canoe that she and her husband used to borrow from Dad to go fishing and sightseeing with. My other sisters chose household items and other things that they had not seen in years.

In my fifties now, I'm the *baby* of the family. I was born seven years after my youngest sister. Partly because of the age differences, each of us had different memories of growing up. I was always interested in airplanes and aviation, so my Dad's occupation always held a particular interest for me. I read the *Lockheed Star* company newspaper with my Dad, and we talked about all of the aircraft that he could talk about with me at the time. When we saw the retirement picture of my Dad in the garage above the workbench, all my siblings agreed that I should be the one to keep it.

As I stood and admired it, I noticed the small numbered stamps near the coworkers signatures. I remembered seeing my Dad's own rubber stamp when he brought it home at the end of his last day at work. I searched through his toolbox and found the stamp in a small drawer containing a few precision gauges. My siblings, having grown and left the house before me, had no idea what I had found. I showed them the stamps on the picture and then showed them Dad's stamp and explained how the stamp was symbolic of Dad's professional approval.

Once we decided who wanted what, we shipped our new treasures back to our homes many miles away, but I carried the small rubber stamp back with me in my pocket on the plane. I keep it in a drawer in my toolbox—just like my dad did. It probably won't mean that much to my two sons, but they know what it means to me.

Tim Egenes is a maintenance manager who has worked in various manufacturing facilities in Northwest Georgia. He and his wife, Kristinn, enjoy boating and taking the motorcycle out for a spin on sunny days. They have two grown sons—Caleb and Andrew.

THE BLUE DIARY

SHANNON LUCADANO

It is hard for me to say that one particular keepsake or memento is more special than the others. I'm the sentimental type who keeps the occasional movie ticket stub because of the time, the person, or the reason behind the occasion. So over the years, I have accumulated a variety of miscellaneous items in various boxes.

I would say that my collecting began the year I decided to keep a diary. I am not sure what motivated me to buy the diary—maybe it was the books we read in school at the time with their main characters who kept diaries. Maybe girls were expected to.

It is blue, etched with a gold border and gold lettering stating "One-Year Diary." I managed to squeeze two years on the pages, because I took a break away from it at one point when my eleven-year-old life had nothing exciting to write about. I guess at age twelve, life became interesting again.

It has a lock on the side and once had a key, though I lost it years ago.

On several occasions, I have gone back through this diary and read through the entries. Half is written in pen, which is great for preserving the thoughts, although my handwriting and spelling was poor at times. The other half is in pencil, because I must have learned some things should not be written down in permanent ink.

I began writing in my diary in September—just a few weeks before I turned eleven. I wrote where I bought it and how much it cost. I have no idea if the store is still in business.

When I turn to the page of my birthday, it says that Granny called wishing me a happy birthday. She said I might not be eleven again. Wow. If she only knew!

I read these pages and still cringe at the words of the time when my preteen angst and puberty was setting in. I had just started a new school, moving out of my childhood neighborhood that fall, so all was new and overwhelming in my life then, as my parents struggled to make ends meet.

The diary also takes me to a time when I only worried about homework, snow days, and if my hairstyle made me look too old—fourteen was ancient. It also mentions the trends of the time as I struggled to be like everyone else (twist beads, anyone?) The TV shows, music and stars of the time are forever recorded with that certain awe that I can still feel when I read the entries.

I laugh, cry and blush at some of the things that went on during the early days of my journaling. This particular book has the honor of being the first of many journals I have kept in my life and, sadly, the one I would choose to keep, as others of my life don't seem as worthy.

So while my time in my mid teens and early twenties are hit and miss with my journals, this little blue diary will always take me back to where—yes, Granny—I might be eleven again.

Shannon enjoys everything nostalgic, loves seeing old photographs, and reads real people's life stories. She's traveled to visit the homesites of her girlhood inspiration for journaling—Laura Ingalls Wilder—by visiting Laura's Little Town on the Praire in DeSmet, South Dakota and Laura's last home with Almanzo in Mansfield, Missouri.

JEMARIS' PURPLE CUP

CARMEN SLAUGHTER

Jemaris Nowell Slaughter was my sister-in-law. More importantly, she was my friend. On paper we could not have been more different. I grew up in the suburbs of Atlanta as a member of a traditional two-parent household. She was raised by a single mother in one of the city's more notorious housing projects, East Lake Meadows. I still chuckle when I think about the number of times she stated, "I cleaned up good but I'm still from the Meadows." I always felt like I would be safe if ever we got caught in any sort of altercation.

Jemaris and I did not bond instantly, but we eventually found common ground during our engagements and subsequent marriages to the Slaughter brothers. Our homes were less than five miles apart and we spent a lot of family time together.

Despite our different backgrounds, hobbies, and personalities, we respected each other and forged a true friendship.

On December 22, 1996, I gave birth to my son, Myles, and in July 1997 Jemaris gave birth to his cousin, Terrence. Our relationship deepened as we shared the joys and pains of pregnancy as well as the excitement of motherhood. We were thrilled that our boys would grow up together and looked forward to seeing them spend time with their fathers, who were both ecstatic at having more Slaughter men in the family. Jemaris also had another son from a previous relationship.

She was determined to become a really great cook with her main goal being to learn how to prepare an awesome Thanksgiving dinner. She dreamed about a time in the future when her boys would bring their girlfriends home for the holidays.

My family has a tradition of eating Thanksgiving dinner at my grandmother's house, so my only responsibility was cooking a side dish and a dessert. For three years, I spent Thanksgiving Eve in the kitchen with Jemaris. We drank and chatted while I watched her experiment with various dishes for her holiday meal. I always had a glass—or two—or three—of wine. Jemaris didn't prefer wine. She drank her brandy cocktails from a purple Tupperware cup.

We shared many secrets and dreams on those nights together. I still remember how we laughed until we cried over silly things and how our husbands would shout from downstairs asking if we were okay. In retrospect, most of the silly things we laughed about were related to those guys.

One Saturday in March 2000, my brother-in-law and Jemaris—with a cocktail in her purple cup—stopped by to visit. After our husbands went outside to do whatever it is men do, Jemaris said she needed some advice.

I poured myself a glass of wine and we talked—*for hours.* At some point we sent the fellas out for takeout and we talked some more. We were both going through trying times in our marriages, and it felt good to have a confidant.

Much, much later that night, they left, and at some point, I noticed Jemaris had left her cup in my sink. As I washed the dishes I thought about our time together and realized how much we had grown to care for one another. We were young mothers trying to find our way and do what was best for our families. I left the purple cup on the counter top, so I would remember to return it to Jemaris the next time I saw her, but I never got that opportunity.

The following Friday as Jemaris and Terrence were on their way home, a hit and run driver struck their vehicle. She did not survive the accident. It was a terrible tragedy that took a mother away from her sons, a wife from her husband, a daughter from her parents, a sister from her brother, and a friend from a friend. The accident took away my friend.

The days and weeks after her death were troubling for me. I questioned why, and I kept thinking how easily it could have been me who died in the accident. Myles and I spent a lot of time traveling to and from Atlanta to my hometown—a distance of almost fifty miles. But the night Jemaris died, she was less than five miles from her home.

I recognized that nothing I could think or feel would change the circumstances, but still, I longed for her.

I do not recall the exact moment I started drinking from her purple cup. All I know is that I did, and I use it whenever I drink a cold beverage.

My marriage ended in 2004, and I decided to move home. When I started to pack my things, I wrapped the purple cup first. It has been twelve years since Jemaris died, but I think about her every single day. I like to think that I have made her proud with my choices—with my life. I feel certain she knows how honored I feel to have known her and loved her. I feel it whenever I drink from her purple cup.

Carmen Tanner Slaughter comes from a long line of storytellers. She spends her days in the classroom and her evenings in pursuit of the perfect sentence.

THE LINDE STAR NECKLACE

THELMA J. BENNER

Twice lost and twice found, this is a story about my treasured keepsakes—my blue sapphire Linde Star necklace and ring. I keep these keepsakes in a butterfly-shaped box from Avon with the inscription "Happiness is like a butterfly. It settles upon you when you least expect it."

I married at seventeen and had five children. After sixteen years, my marriage ended in divorce. I was determined to make a better life for me and my children, so I pursued my dream of becoming a nurse.

The nearby Good Samaritan Hospital in Lebanon, Pennsylvania offered a one year course and was within walking distance. After much planning and with the help of dear neighbors and beloved family members, I started LPN School in February 1967 and graduated in February 1968—all to God's glory.

THE LINDE STAR NECKLACE

I got a position at the Good Samaritan Hospital on the night shift from 11:00 p.m. to 7:00 a.m., which is the shift I preferred so I could be home with my children during the day. The pay was not much. I knew that when I passed the state board test in July, I would get a raise, but until then, we lived on a very tight budget, and I needed a second job.

My dear friend, Joe Miller owed Achenbach's Restaurant in Hershey, Pennsylvania and offered me a part-time waitressing job. This was a new experience for me. I truly enjoyed the work and the money was a big help, but juggling my work and family was not easy. When the older children were in school, I catnapped on the sofa while my four-year-old son played. I also slept a few hours after supper when the older children were home from school. We all worked together with our schedules. I often worked from 3 p.m. to 10 p.m. at the restaurant, then went to the hospital from 11 p.m. to 7 a.m. with little or no sleep.

One day while at the restaurant, I thumbed through a catalog that Joe ordered from each month and noticed a Linde Star necklace and matching ring. The pendant was a brilliant blue gem with a Linde Star's distinctive sharp white starfish pattern. It dangled on a silver chain. The ring had the same beautiful gem. It was a magnificent jewelry ensemble, and although I always wanted a Linde Star necklace, such a luxury was never in my budget. After all, I was a single mother raising five children and barely had enough money to pay our bills, purchase food, and buy the necessities of life.

"Maybe if I saved my tips from waitressing I could afford the set," I thought. I was thrilled with the idea and asked Joe to put it on his next order for my birthday present in April 1970.

But Joe had a surprise for me. When the necklace and ring finally arrived, Joe said, "It's your birthday present from me!"

I was so happy. I hugged him, kissed him, and told him that it was the first thing in my life that I really wanted but didn't have to pay for myself. It was a special moment.

I wore the necklace and ring all the time—admiring it with each glance.

One afternoon several years later, I reached up to touch the smooth stone on my chest and realized it was gone. I was heartsick. *"It's just a material thing,"* I told myself. *"It can be replaced."*

But the necklace held a special place in my heart. It was more than a necklace. It had become a priceless keepsake, and losing it was too hard to accept. I prayed and turned the house upside-down looking for it. I even crawled on the floors. I finally found it close to the side of my desk, lodged deeply in the carpet. I was so overwhelmed that my prayers had been answered, and to prevent another loss, I bought a new chain with a safety clasp for my Linde Star sapphire.

But that is not the end of my keepsake story. Several years later, my family and I spent a day at the Hershey Amusement Park riding roller coasters and spinning around the twirly rides. After we got home, I lay down to take a nap and discovered my beloved necklace was gone again. With tears and prayers I cried, *"How could this happen again?"*

I believed it had fallen off at the park and didn't think I would ever see it or feel it against my chest again.

"So be it," I thought as I calmed myself. *"It's not the end of the world—it's just a necklace."*

Months went by, then one evening as I made my bed, I noticed something that looked like a piece of tinsel embedded in a hand-crocheted throw pillow. I tugged at the silver object and realized it was my Linde Star necklace.

I literally cried and jumped with joy. I thanked God for helping me find my Linde Star keepsake yet again.

For several months I dwelled on the loss and improbable, miraculous recoveries of my Linde Star necklace and had a revelation—perhaps God was teaching me not to put material things above what is most important in life.

I stopped wearing the necklace and ring, but to this day, I still treasure them—keeping them safely stowed in the butterfly box on my bureau.

My dear friend Joe passed away in March 2012. Sometimes I hold the necklace and look at the blue stone with its fantastic starburst pattern and remember his kindness during a very difficult time in my life. The memory is as beautiful as the necklace itself.

Over the decades, the necklace has brought special meaning to my life—reminding me that in life, things that seem lost can often be found again through effort and perseverance. Most of all, the keepsake is a symbol of faith—a reminder that we should trust in God for He is in control of all things and as Psalms 37:4 says, "He will give us the desire of our hearts."

Originally from Pennsylvania, Thelma J. Benner is a retired nurse who lives with her daughter in Northwest Georgia. She enjoys reading and writing poetry, and she keeps in touch with family and friends throughout the United States.

CASTANETS

DEBBIE DICKSON

Castanets are percussion instruments associated with Spanish music. The instruments consist of pairs of hollowed-out pieces of wood joined on one edge by a string. Musicians and dancers hold the castanets in their hands and produce clicking sounds for rhythmic accents.

But at my house, castanets served another purpose. They were used for teaching Spanish, and for that reason, castanets remind me of my mother, Joy Schwamb Dickson.

After my sister and I both began junior high and grade school, respectively, Mom returned to college and graduated Suma Cum Laude with a major in English and minor in Spanish. She continued her studies and soon majored in Spanish as well.

Mom became a teacher and taught Spanish I and II and

English II at Wilcox County High School in South Georgia. She was one of those teachers who loved teaching with all her heart and loved her students, too. My father, Hal Dickson, taught also (eleventh grade literature and photography), but it was mom's love for the profession that always stood out.

Family dinner conversations revolved around the happenings of the day from the grammar school, junior high school, and high school. Many evenings, Mom shared stories from her high school classroom, as I laughed uncontrollably. You see, Mom was very intelligent, but *gullible*. Her students adored her, and as a result, they picked on her, teased her, and played jokes on her, but she took it all very well. She had an easy-going, kind nature about her.

I remember one time, Wen Howell, the son of the local pharmacist, reported to Mom's Spanish class unprepared for the scheduled exam. He convinced my mother that he had found his beloved dog dead and was much too upset to study the night before. Mom, being the believer in people that she was, of course, allowed Wen to postpone his exam. However, in the next days, Wen's story unraveled and the truth emerged—the family dog had *not* died. Mr. Wendell was as red faced as I had ever seen him when he got wind of his son's tall tale.

Another story involved a boy named, Tim Rutherford. My mom had a beehive hairdo when the style was popular and made weekly trips to the beauty shop to have the top of her *hive* attached—as they say—to her hair. The day prior to one of her hair appointments, Tim Rutherford followed Mom around her classroom with hands stretched out behind her like he was racing to catch a fly ball, all the while reassuring her that he would catch her beehive if it fell off. Every time I visualize Tim running around behind my mother in class, I smile.

And so, my childhood was filled with story after story of Mom's adventures in teaching.

Mom used castanets as a teaching tool in her Spanish classes, so we always had castanet pairs scattered throughout our house. They became fixtures of my youth. Even when my sister and I were grown and had children of our own, our children would find a pair in my parents' home, walk over to my mother and plead, "Show me how, Grandma."

Mom couldn't resist her grandchildren. For the next half an hour or so, she gave them her undivided attention—putting the castanets in her hands, then in their little hands, and clicking. She showed them how to use them to develop correct accent and annunciation of the Spanish language, simultaneously.

In 1995, when Mom was diagnosed with metastatic breast cancer, her doctors urged her to take a medical leave of absence from teaching while undergoing chemotherapy treatments. There was nothing doing where Mom was concerned. Teaching was her life, and she had no intentions of stopping, even for a little while.

The next year, Mom taught Mondays through Thursdays without fail—Fridays were devoted to chemo treatments. The 140-mile-round-trip Fridays were tiring for Mom, but the exhaustion was not enough to push her to give up her classroom. Indeed, many of those Fridays, Dad was Mom's substitute teacher. And so she continued to teach and nurture her students.

But the second year of her battle was different—it was much more difficult. Mom decided it was finally time to pass the teaching torch on to a predecessor. But retiring from teaching left a hole in her heart, and she sorely missed her students.

One day several months later, I walked through Mom's room while she napped and witnessed her—eyes closed, right hand held high with index finger pointing into the air—correcting her students in her sleep.

"NO, NO, NO!" she said with a smile.

Even as cancer ravaged her body, she continued to *teach* in her dreams using perfect Spanish and accent, which was all she allowed spoken in her classroom after the first few classes. I saw her teaching in her sleep often that year—watched her hands working an imaginary pair of castanets. It was a true testament of her love of being an educator.

Years have passed since I lost my mother, yet I still feel her presence all around me, especially when I see her castanets, which Dad still keeps around the house. When I see them, I remember their *click, click, click* and the perfection of Mom's voice. I see clearly the memory of her teaching her grandchildren how to speak and how to play. And I'm reminded of her boundless love of teaching—a calling that brought joy to her glorious life for so many years.

Debbie Dickson is a mother of three and grandmother of three. She is a nursing supervisor in Georgia who loves her job and enjoys cooking, reading, and most of all, spending time with family and friends.

WRITING ABOUT KEEPSAKES

Welcome to *Project Keepsake*—a collection of keepsake stories told in first person by both writers and nonwriters about their treasured keepsakes. I personally encourage you to write about one of your own keepsakes, and I personally invite you to submit your story and become a *Project Keepsake* contributor.

Having read and written dozens of keepsake stories, I can offer some sound advice on how to develop a compelling story. But before we get started, please consider the following:

- *Project Keepsake* stories are true, narrative nonfiction pieces written in first person.
- *Project Keepsake* stories are typically 800 to 2500 words in length.
- *Project Keepsake* stories have depth to them. The writer explores and reveals his feelings, emotions, and thoughts as the story unfolds.
- *Project Keepsake* stories are original works and haven't been previously published. So, let's get started.

1. IDENTIFY A KEEPSAKE OR MEMENTO

First, you'll need to select a keepsake in your possession. What? Oh, I know you have one—or two or three or four. Most of us hold onto a few objects because they remind us of loved ones, significant moments, or places we don't want to forget. Keepsakes, mementos, souvenirs, and heirlooms are very similar. A keepsake is something with sentimental value. A memento is a reminder of a past event. A souvenir is a thing kept as a reminder of a person, place, or event. An heirloom is an object that has belonged to a family member. So by definition—and from my perspective—mementos, souvenirs, and heirlooms are all keepsakes.

Dozens of remnants from my life surround me in my own home comforting me like a warm, cozy blanket. For example:

- A framed knife graces the wall of the breakfast room and reminds me of both a memorable vacation and my father. My husband and I purchased the knife as a souvenir for him on a trip to Greece almost two decades ago.
- In my office, a glass vase hangs by a chain from the finial of a curtain rod. This beautiful purple piece once hung in a sunroom window of my parents-in-law's eclectically decorated home—casting pinkish-purplish, prismatic beams of light onto their black and white checkered floor. I can't look at the vase without thinking of them.
- An old tin, windup toy—a white bunny riding a tricycle—sits atop a dresser in the bedroom, reminding me of Roxy, a lovable, long-haired German Shepherd. One Easter, my husband wound the toy and placed it on the floor in front of our beloved dog. The clanging toy terrified Roxy, and she raced from the room as if it were chasing her. After Roxy died in 2001, the simple toy was transformed into something powerful—a keepsake connecting us to a fond memory of her.

Look on your shelves, in your closets, under beds, in your drawers, in storage boxes, on your walls, and in your curio cabinet. Browse around your home until you find a keepsake you want to write about.

2. BRAINSTORM

Hold your keepsake in your hand, or position your body so that you can study your keepsake. Equipped with several sheets of blank paper and a pen, write everything that flows into your mind pertaining to your keepsake. Keep writing thoughts for at least ten minutes.

If thoughts and memories don't flood your mind, jog your brain by asking yourself these questions:

- What is the keepsake?
- Where did the keepsake come from?
- How long have I had it?
- What does it look like?
- What does it smell like?
- What does it sound like?
- What does it feel like?
- Why is it special or significant to me?
- What and/or whom does it remind me of, and why?
- Why do I keep it?
- Are there any stories about the keepsake? If so, what are they?
- How does the keepsake make me feel, and why?
- Where do I keep this keepsake, and why?
- Does the item have monetary value, and if so, how much?
- What are my plans for the keepsake? For example, do I plan to pass it on to a friend or family member some day? If so, who, and why?

3. ORGANIZE YOUR THOUGHTS

Organizing your thoughts and your story is much like charting a course on a map before you leave on a long trip—it helps you stay on course and prevents you from making a wrong turn and getting lost in your own words.

There are many ways to organize your thoughts. My two favorite techniques are bubbling diagrams and outlines.

Below, I've presented both an outline and a bubble diagram of a story about another one of my keepsakes. Here's a little background—years ago, my husband and I visited the Pennsylvania Amish country. While we were there, we commissioned an artist to recreate a scene in pastels similar to a piece we saw at a gallery in Lancaster County. The piece has been a centerpiece of our dining room ever since.

An Outline—"Amish and English"

An outline shows the order of the various topics, the relative importance of each, and the relationship between the various parts.

  I. Introduction—I'll take readers to the Pennsylvania Amish Country as Gene and I roamed around Lancaster County and the surrounding countryside
  A. Horse-drawn buggies on roads
  B. Men plowing fields with mules
  C. Pristine countrysides and dirt roads
  D. Quilts flapping on the clotheslines
  E. Who are the Amish?
   1. They are Godly people who believe in living in traditional manners
   2. Strict regulations pertaining to power-line electricity, telephones, automobiles, and clothing

3. They value simple rural life, manual labor, and humility
II. Gallery
   A. We were looking for a souvenir for ourselves
   B. We wandered into the gallery
   C. Dozens of pieces by J.G. McGill
III. Seeing the artwork—"English and Amish"
   A. Pastels—the art looked fuzzy up-close but very detailed from a distance
   B. "English and Amish" referred to contrasting subjects in the piece
      1. The Amish—Amish children running across a dirt road.
      2. The English—Amish call non-Amish people, Englishmen. In the upper right corner is a contrail from the modern world—a subtle reminder of the English (non-Amish) world.
   C. We instantly fell in love with the piece because it was beautiful, colorful, lively, and a perfect reminder of our vacation
   D. $800 for the framed piece
IV. Decision
   A. Because it was so much money, we decided to leave and think about it overnight
   B. Over dinner, we decided to purchase "English and Amish"
   C. When we went back to the gallery the next day, the piece was gone. It had been sold to another customer, and we were heart broken.
V. Commissioned Art
   A. The gallery owner called the artist and arranged for him to paint us a similar scene and send us photos.

WRITING ABOUT KEEPSAKES

B. Six weeks later, we received photos in the mail. The piece was different, but as beautiful as the piece we had seen at the gallery.

C. We sent him a check, and he sent us "Amish and English."

Bubble Diagram—"Amish and English"

The bubble method—or bubbling—is a graphical way to brainstorm and organize thoughts. To create a bubble chart, summarize your topic in one word or phrase, write it on a paper, and circle it. Then write down all ideas associated with it around the main topic. Circle each of these ideas and draw a line from them to the main topic. Do the same thing with each of the additional ideas, making sure that you stay within the scope of the main topic. Write down each of the additional ideas that each idea brings to mind, circle them and draw a line back to the first idea that brought that one to mind. Your diagram will look something like this:

4. START WRITING

Now that you've created a roadmap of your story, you are ready to begin your writing journey.

First, title your story using the name of your keepsake (i.e. *My Silver Locket, The Big Yellow Fishing Lure, George's Glasses, The Heart-Shaped Ashtray, An Afghan from Grandmother Jarriel*). The title will cue the reader and allow you to plunge right into your story without first defining your keepsake or memento.

Next, develop a strong beginning to your story to *hook* your audience. Consider beginning your keepsake story with an action or a short interesting anecdote. Take the reader back to an interesting scene in your life that relates to your keepsake or introduces your keepsake. Make the reader feel he is there with you.

For example, the following sentence is a rather blah and boring beginning:

> I keep my dad's old Atlanta Braves baseball cap hanging on a hook in my laundry room.

Perhaps a better way to start the story about my father's baseball cap is to take the reader back to a game where my dad wore the cap. For example:

> With two outs in the bottom of the ninth inning, the fate of the season rested on Dale Murphy's shoulders as he stepped up to the plate and started his routine of practice swings. The stadium rocked and roared as fans chanted the Atlanta Braves' battle cry and made tomahawk chopping motions with their right arms, in unison. I shifted nervously in my seat then looked over at my dad—his pale blue eyes glued to the batter. He removed his faded old Braves

baseball cap and blotted summery beads of sweat from his brow with a white handkerchief that he kept in his pocket.

Using dialogue is another great way to hook your reader and make your writing shine. One keepsake story contributor—Priscilla Shartle—started her story with powerful dialogue that demands the reader's immediate and full attention. Her story opens with:

"Mama's dead!"
For a few seconds I wasn't sure if I was dreaming or awake. I remember hearing the telephone ring and glancing at the clock on the bedside table. It was 7:30 a.m., Monday, April 1, 1991. It was my sister's voice on the other end of the line, but surely Mama wasn't dead.
"What do you mean, Mama's dead?" I asked. The telephone seemed to weigh a ton as I held it tightly to my ear.
"Well, I think she is," Lindy added.
I thought, "This is an April Fool's joke, and not a funny one."
Finally I got her to tell me that Daddy had called her and said Mama had died in her sleep. Lindy was at my parents' apartment in Baton Rouge, Louisiana. I was in Winston-Salem, North Carolina at my home.
"Have you seen Mama?" I asked.
Lindy replied, "No."
My frustration and fear of what she was saying began to sink in and my temper flared. I screamed into the phone, ordering my sister to go see and make sure Mama really was dead.

Some times, an opening paragraph ties into a closing thought presented in the final paragraph. For example, keepsake story contributor, Mitzi Boyd opened her story with:

> As a child, I knew that I could count on my Nanny Keith for numerous things that I might need.

And at the end of her story, she revisits the opening by writing:

> *Nanny left the magic for me in the pan after all—another thing I just knew I could count on her for.*

Try several different opening paragraphs and select the strongest one.

Now that you've started your story with strong action, powerful dialogue, or imagery, keep it going. Use your outline or bubble diagram as a guide, and just write. Be bold, be fearless, and resist the urge to edit your work until you get all—or most—of your story on paper.

5. EDIT YOUR STORY

After you draft your story, edit it. Slowly read your story out loud and fix problems. Make sure your subjects and verbs agree. Check for consistent verb tense usage. Look at spelling, capitalization, punctuation, and grammar. Remove unnecessary words, sentences, and paragraphs. Search for stronger, *stickier* words to replace dull, lackluster words. Think about the sequence of events in your story and consider moving paragraphs around to make the story flow better.

There are several secrets that professional writers use to polish their writing. Try some of these tricks to spice up your story.

- Add interesting descriptions from your senses. Think about how things looked, smelled, sounded, and felt and rewrite some of your sentences.

WRITING ABOUT KEEPSAKES

Draft: The *cabin* was near the *river*
Revision: The *little log cabin near the roaring river smelled like fish, pine, and decaying leaves.*

- Use strong, dynamic action verbs.

Draft: Sheena *ran* from the house.
Revision: Sheena *bolted* from the house.

Draft: Herman *shut* the front door.
Revision: Herman *slammed* the front door.

Draft: Michelle *threw* her diamond engagement ring at Buck's head.
Revision: Michelle *flung* her diamond engagement ring at Buck's head.

- Use dialogue in your story, if appropriate, and use words and phrases representative of the individual's language patterns to make your story more authentic.

Draft: My dad had a fear of snakes.
Revision: "Snakes are evil," my dad often said. "The only good snake is a dead snake."

Draft: My sister called and told me Yancey had died.
Revision: "Hey, I called with bad news," my sister said. "Yancey died this morning."
    I gasped, then collected myself and asked, "How did he die?"
    "Some type of respiratory problem," she answered.

Draft: My grandmother told me Nell had moved to Savannah.
Revision: "Nell moved to Savanner," my grandmother reported. Grandmother was educated in a poor, rural area of South Georgia,

and she commonly changed the pronunciations of words—Savannah became Savanner, banana was bananer, Everett sounded like Evert, and pretty was pronounced purdy.

- Include your thoughts.

Draft: Watching the towers fall on September 11th made me sad and uncertain.
Revision: Watching the towers fall filled me with great despair, and I wondered, "Is this the end of the world as I have known it? Will my nieces and nephews live in a world filled with fear, terror, and hatred?"

6. SET IT ASIDE

After you edit your keepsake story, set it aside and let it simmer for a week. Move onto other things and try not to think about your story.

7. EDIT AGAIN

Read your story again, and edit it one more time. Share your story with a friend or another writer and ask him for his suggestions. Consider the suggestions and then edit again.

8. FORMAT, NAME, AND PACKAGE

Format, name, and package your keepsake story as follows:

- Use 1" margins on all sides of the document.
- Use black, Times New Roman, size 12 font.
- Double space your entire document.
- Position your title at the center top of the page in all caps.

- On the next line, type "by" in the center.
- Starting on the third line, type and center your full name, address, phone number, and email address.
- Start your story on the fourth line left justified with 5 space indentions at the beginning of each paragraph.
- Include page numbers on the lower right footer (i.e. page 2 of 4).
- At the end of your story, include a brief bio (fifty to seventy-five words) about yourself (i.e. Freelance writer Amber Lanier Nagle lives in a house full of keepsakes and mementos. When she isn't writing, she enjoys reading on the front porch, planting flowers and vegetables in her garden, and hiking the picturesque trails of Northwest Georgia. She and her husband, Gene, live in the woods with three big dogs, wandering rafters of wild turkeys, and occasional ring-tailed raccoons, deer and possums.)
- Save as a Microsoft Word document, Mac Pages document, or a pdf.
- Rename your file using the name of your keepsake, an underscore, your first name, and your last name with no spaces (i.e. FishingLure_AndyLanier, IrishTrunk_MargaretCooney, OrnateVase_JenniferPritchard).

9. CONTRIBUTE YOUR STORY

Upload your story on the *Project Keepsake* web site at www.ProjectKeepsake.com, or compose an email to me (Amber@AmberNagle.com) with *Project Keepsake* in the Subject line. Attach your file to the email. Also, if you have a clear, high resolution photo of your keepsake, attach your photo, too. Include your contact information in the body of the email and send it. I will respond to your message at my earliest convenience.

Before you send me your keepsake story, please consider the following:

- By contributing your story to *Project Keepsake*, you are gifting your story to me, Amber Lanier Nagle, and allowing me to include your story (with your byline) in my collection of keepsake stories without compensation.
- By contributing your story to *Project Keepsake*, you are allowing me, Amber Lanier Nagle, to use your story (with your byline) to market the project on the Internet, on radio, on television, at conferences, at meetings, at workshops, via podcasts, etc., without compensation.

10. TELL YOUR FAMILY AND FRIENDS

Project Keepsake is a work in progress with three simple goals: to get aspiring writers to put their pen to paper and try their hand at writing, to get more people interested in the art of storytelling, and to record the many stories associated with keepsakes and mementos. Help us promote the project by encouraging your family and friends to visit the *Project Keepsake* web site (www.ProjectKeepsake.com) and write a story or two about their own keepsakes.

WITH SINCERE GRATITUDE

I would like to thank my parents, Herman and Wanda Lanier, who taught me that connections and relationships with other people matter in this world, and that life has greater meaning when we recognize the singular moments—the joyous, the mundane, and tragic—that give lifetimes their cyclical definition.

Thank you to my husband, Gene Nagle, who has always supported my efforts to write—even when the writing assignments were merely trickling in, and even though I went to engineering school. Thanks, Gene, for believing in me.

Thank you to each of my *Project Keepsake* contributors for writing beautiful keepsake stories and allowing me to use them in the first collection. A very special thanks to my *Project Keepsake* pioneers—David Aft, Mitzi Boyd, Dana Cooley-Keith, Shannon Lucadano, Wayne Minshew, Tim Egenes, Bob Wright, Janie Aker, Martha Buttrum, Jane Starner, and Sharon Huey. This group of friends and associates sent stories to me immediately after I explained the project to them. They seemed to love my idea from the very beginning, cheered me on, and even recruited other contributors to participate in the project. I appreciate all of you more than you know.

WITH SINCERE GRATITUDE

Thanks to the family and friends who have listened to me go on and on and on about *Project Keepsake* in the last two years—the work, the rejections, the doubt, the encouraging news, etc. I appreciate your patience, and I hope to repay your kindness one day.

Finally, thank you to the many readers and followers of *Project Keepsake*. For us writers, it is such a thrill when someone enjoys reading the words we've slaved over. Thank you so much, and stay tuned for more keepsake stories.

ABOUT THE EDITOR

Amber Lanier Nagle is a freelance writer based in Georgia. She's published articles in *Grit*, *Mother Earth News*, *Points North*, and many other magazines. When she isn't writing, Nagle spends time outdoors with her husband and works with aspiring writers.

INTEGRATED MEDIA

Find a full list of our authors and
titles at www.openroadmedia.com

FOLLOW US
@OpenRoadMedia

Printed in the USA
CPSIA information can be obtained
at www.ICGtesting.com
LVHW041232100424
776743LV00003B/165

9 781504 079433